G000320209

Decorative Dough Craft

Decorative Dough Craft

Beautiful Projects for Different Occasions

Lynne Langfeld

COLLINS & BROWN

ACKNOWLEDGEMENTS

I would like to thank all my family for their help and support during the preparation of this book, especially my mother for giving me such encouragement and inspiration.

I would like to dedicate this book to my lovely children, Marie-Claire, Anna-Sophie and Johann Sebastian.

First published in Great Britain in 1996 by
Collins & Brown Limited
London House
Great Eastern Wharf
Parkgate Road
London SW11 4NQ

Copyright © Collins & Brown Limited
Text copyright © Collins & Brown Limited 1996
Photographs copyright © Collins & Brown Limited 1996
Illustrations copyright © Collins & Brown Limited 1996

The right of Lynne Langfeld to be identified as the author of this work has been asserted by her in accordance with the Copyright, Designs and Patents Act, 1988.

All rights reserved. No part of this publication may be reproduced, stored in a retrieval system, or transmitted in any form or by any means electronic, mechanical, photocopying, recording or otherwise, without the prior written permission of the publisher.

1 3 5 7 9 8 6 4 2

British Library Cataloguing in Publication Data:

A catalogue record for this book is available from the British Library

ISBN 1 85470 248 3 (hardback edition)
ISBN 1 85585 402 3 (paperback edition)

Editor: Gillian Haslam
Designer: Alison Shackleton
Photography: Shona Wood
Cover design: Christine Wood

Reproduction by Bright Art, Singapore
Printed and bound by L.E.G.O., Italy

Contents

Introduction

Although we perhaps consider modelling dough as something relatively new, it is in fact a very ancient craft. Long ago at harvest time, peasants made decorations for their homes out of dough as symbols of thanks for their daily bread. In old Mexican traditions, dough figures were made for burials and placed in coffins to ward away evil spirits. Native American fertility symbols were also traditionally made of dough and given as gifts. Even nowadays, on the island of Crete wedding wreaths of dough beautifully decorated with leaves and flowers are given as good luck charms to the happy couple.

A craft similar to these age-old traditions is becoming more and more popular in today's modern world. However, contemporary dough craft uses salt dough, which is like bread but contains no yeast. It is made with a high quantity of salt which prevents the decorations you make from going mouldy.

The beauty of modelling with salt dough is that you will need to buy no special ingredients or equipment at all. Everything you could possibly need for making and modelling the dough you will probably find in your kitchen. The techniques are easy to learn and it is an ideal hobby for the family. My own children have thoroughly enjoyed helping me with this book. Given some dough, extra water and flour, they have amused themselves for hours making tiny things for their doll's house, pictures for their bedrooms and gifts for their friends.

Although some of the ornaments in this book once painted and varnished look difficult to make, you will be surprised just how simple it is. The dough is easy to handle and as it does not dry out too quickly, you can really take your time. With a little patience and imagination there is really no limit to the things you can make. Surprise those friends of yours who have everything with something that little bit different. Above all – have fun!

Design Ideas

Salt dough is a very popular and inexpensive modelling medium. The variety of ornaments you can make is limitless provided you remember a few basic rules. Unlike porcelain or clay, which can be modelled to any size, salt dough is not suitable for large or free-standing objects. The dough, once baked, is quite brittle and ornaments would not be able to stand up to everyday use. You would not, for instance, be able to make vases or cups for holding liquid as the dough would absorb moisture and collapse. However, it is an ideal medium for ornaments such as wall plaques, wreaths, figures or miniatures for dolls' houses.

All the projects in this book are baked, or more precisely dried-out, on oven trays and unfortunately we cannot exceed the size of the oven shelf which again limits the dimensions of salt dough objects. The ornaments in this book vary in size from 18 cm (7 in) for most of the figures, to 30.5 cm (12 in) for the larger wreaths.

Another consideration is that these objects are only suitable for indoors. Due to the high salt content in the dough, the ornaments will absorb any moisture present in the atmosphere, become spongy and eventually disintegrate if they are not kept in a dry environment – no matter how many coats of varnish are given. Therefore they should not be hung on damp walls, in bathrooms and certainly not outside.

I cannot definitely say how long your ornaments will last. I have been modelling now for over 10 years and the very first ornaments I made are still in good condition despite several moves in that time. If your ornaments have been baked and protected properly with varnish, you should have pleasure from them for many years.

INSPIRATION FOR DESIGNS

Inspiration for dough craft designs can be taken from illustrated children's books, history books, from magazines, cookery books and of course from nature itself. In fact anything that catches your eye! Over many years I have compiled scrap books with cut-outs from magazines, birthday and Christmas cards. These contain images of figures, dolls, houses, flowers and trees, animals, folk art, designs for embroidery, samplers, famous pieces of art, and interior design. During the preparation of this book I have referred to these scrap books on many occasions for new ideas. I particularly like the designs in folk art, with their basic shapes and their naïve style of painting. These have inspired my simple designs for the baskets and wreaths, to which I have then tried to add just a little sophistication.

There is such enormous scope for making ornaments out of salt dough, you can really let your imagination run wild. However, if you are choosing or designing something for a specific friend, you should consider his or her taste and style before deciding on a design. Would they appreciate something amusing? Or would they really like something in the peasant style? Or perhaps they would prefer something more sophisticated? The room the ornament is designed for should also be taken into consideration –

kitchen, lounge or bedroom – as should the time of year, if the piece is to reflect seasonal festivities.

Children's bedrooms are fun to design for. A frieze could be made of different sized teddy bears, clowns or favourite characters from films or story books. Try designing your own border of dough characters placed just above a dado rail.

SPECIAL OCCASIONS

Christmas is a special time, and dough craft is perfect for the celebrations. Not only can you entertain your children for hours making Christmas tree decorations, but you can also really put

Try these wall plaques depicting a tree through the four seasons. The base for each plaque is made from dough rolled out directly on to the baking tray to a thickness of 6mm (¼ in). Use a teaplate as a circular template. Cut around the plate and remove the excess dough. Neaten the edges and place a long, thin sausage of dough around the edge as a frame. Adhere the dough trees to the plaques with a little water.

your creative skills to the test making wreaths decorated with holly and berries, swags full of Christmas roses, holly and mistletoe as well as home-made gifts for all your relatives and friends. Try making wall plaques in the shape of Christmas stockings filled with toys and painted bright colours. Or make large snowmen, similar in size to Father Christmas on p.63, or even wall plaques in the form of angels. After baking, simply paint them with gold acrylic paint. With your new skills you can create a whole new look for this festive season. For example, try decorating your tree with fruit, either left natural or painted in bright colours as a pleasant alternative to more traditional decorations.

There are many different occasions to make new and imaginative gifts for. For the next wedding you are invited to, make an extra gift for the bride and groom to remind them of their special day – perhaps a bouquet of flowers for the bride, a lucky horseshoe for the groom, or even small dough figures of the bride and groom, painted to match their wedding outfits.

The birth of a new baby or a christening are other occasions when you could put your new skills to the test. A unique wall plaque for the baby, decorated with a crib or toys and including the date of birth and the baby's and parents' names, makes a special gift.

Don't forget wedding anniversaries, engagements and special 'milestone' birthdays – 40, 60, 80, etc. For friends or family who have just moved house, try making a dough replica of their new home, adding the date when they moved. This makes a lovely, lasting alternative to the more traditional card.

Easter is another very special occasion associated with the traditional images of eggs, spring flowers and Easter bunnies. In this book I have made two projects specifically for Easter. The

Houses make lovely wall plaques. They would make an ideal gift for someone who has just moved, and there are so many different types to choose from – houses, cottages, town-houses, mansions – the choice of design is endless.

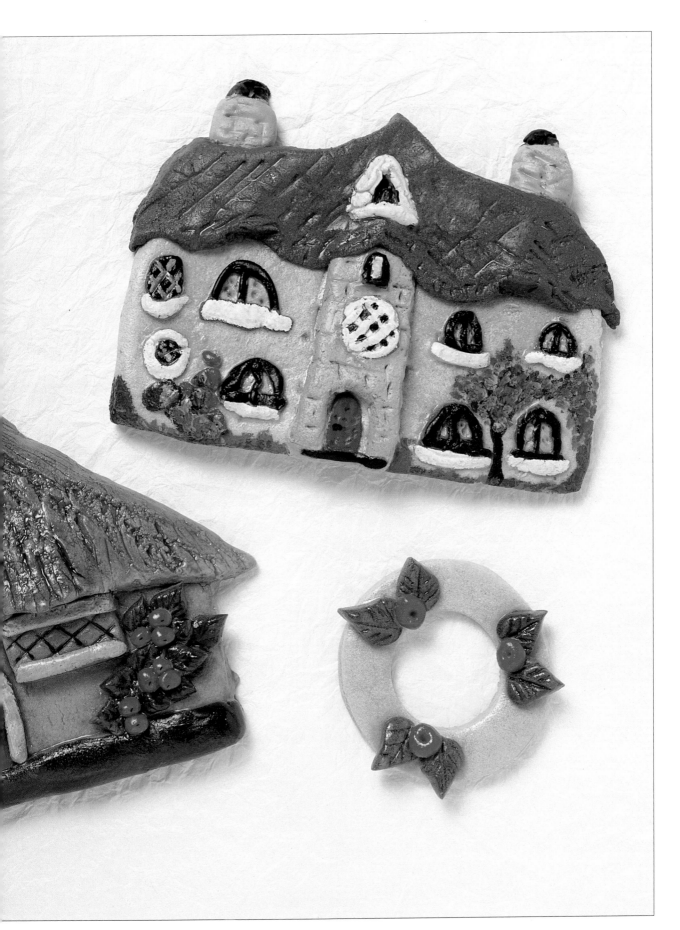

Easter wreath on p.72 can be used for real or chocolate eggs at breakfast time on Easter Sunday. This is quite an easy project and one that children would be able to help you with. The second project is the Easter egg lady on p.75. This amusing, rather stylized and naive figure could decorate your kitchen all year round.

The wheatsheaf on p.77, made for harvest festival or thanksgiving, is in my opinion one of the most effective projects in this book. This worldwide symbol of the harvest, although quite time-consuming, is easy to make. The apple tree shown on p.80 is another project ideal for harvest festival. Once you have mastered the art of making this tree, use your imagination and make another tree filled with spring blossom. You can also create a completely different look by painting the tree in traditional colours after baking.

I have tried to make the projects in this book as varied as possible. Some of them are particularly easy and perhaps more suitable for children or beginners. Others are slightly more complex and can be quite a challenge for even the most experienced adult. The projects which I would recommend for children are the bread, fruits and vegetables for a doll's house (p.60), rocking horse and teddy bear plaques (p.58), and the egg cups (p.104). For adult beginners, try the apple wreath (p.42), the fruit wreath (p.47), or the cock and hen (p.68). Before you start any projects, I recommend you read the chapter on tips and techniques (p.18). Once you have mastered the basic shapes and techniques, you can think up your own projects.

PLANNING AHEAD

Several points are worth bearing in mind before you start. When making ornaments for special occasions such as Christmas, birthdays or Easter, give yourself adequate time and begin well in advance. The actual modelling of most items in the book may take up to two hours; the baking, or more specifically the drying-out process, can take up to four days depending on the size of the ornament (see Tips and Techniques, p.32). Cooling down is also a slow process which can last up to another eight hours.

To decorate your ornaments, the paints I always use are water-based, artist's acrylic paints (poster paints) which should always be given time to dry out thoroughly, preferably overnight. Varnishing is very important and must be done properly. Again, think ahead, as at least two to three days will be needed for the two coats to be applied and to dry out properly. And don't forget to varnish both sides of the ornament after painting.

The different modelling techniques used throughout are described in detail in the Tips and Techniques section, and it would be advisable to read these through before actually beginning any of the projects. The techniques are quite varied and modelling aids such as biscuit cutters, templates and moulds are used to simplify the projects.

I should mention at this stage that it is very important to use relatively new, non-stick baking trays with low sides. High-sided roasting trays can create problems during modelling as the sides

This stylised tree symbolises the tree of life. It has one main central trunk and three long branches on either side, which are folded upwards and joined to the trunk, forming loops. The tree is decorated with fruit, flowers, acorns and even a tiny bird in a nest. It stands 28cm (11 in) tall and at the widest point measures 18cm (7 in).

tend to get in the way when rolling out the dough; and ornaments tend to stick to old, rusty trays, refusing to release themselves from the tin no matter how long you bake them. The trays shown in the step-by-step photographs are ideal.

The baking of your ornaments is probably the most important part of the whole process. Once you have spent so much time and put so much effort into making something, it is very upsetting to ruin it at this stage. You must remember that unlike pastry or cakes, salt dough needs to 'dry out' rather than 'bake'. If your oven is too hot, blisters will appear on the surface of the ornament and large cracks will form on the underside. Again, it is important that you become familiar with the baking techniques before starting (see Tips and Techniques p.32).

Finally, decorating and painting your ornaments can completely transform them and it is at this stage that you can really personalize them and add that little extra touch. Some projects are better suited to a natural look which can be enhanced with a 'high-baked effect' described in Tips and Techniques. Others look better painted in bright colours to make them more striking or give them more character. Whichever look you choose, don't forget to finish off and protect your ornaments by varnishing them properly.

This delightful choir, complete with choirmaster in red robes and with a glowing lantern, makes a special decoration for Christmas. See p.87 for instructions for making these and many other festive ornaments.

Tips and Techniques

The great thing about salt dough is that it is just about the cheapest modelling medium of all — all the ingredients and utensils required for mixing and modelling the dough you will probably already have in your kitchen! In this section you can find all you need to know about salt dough recipes, modelling techniques, and useful hints for special effects, as well as methods of baking, painting, varnishing, repairing and storing.

BASIC RECIPE

The following recipe makes up approximately 1 kg (2 lbs) of salt dough.

Either using scales or a standard small beaker, measure out:
350 g (12 oz) = 2 beakers plain flour
350 g (12 oz) = 1 beaker salt
225 ml (½ pint) water = 1 beaker water

RECIPE VARIATIONS

Wholemeal flour
Instead of strong white flour, you can use wholemeal bread flour. Wholemeal flour gives a speckled appearance when baked which can create a more rustic look. However, it is slightly less pliable than white flour when modelling.

To make brown dough
Either add 20ml (2 tablespoons) of gravy browning to the water before mixing the ingredients together, or mix a bouillon cube with hot water, then allow the water to cool before mixing in the flour and salt.

> ### TIP
> If you have sensitive skin you might want to wear rubber gloves when mixing the dough. The high salt content in the dough does tend to dry out the skin, and you should always have the hand cream ready after modelling.

> ### TIPS
>
> **Flour**
> You can use the cheapest brand of flour, but do not use self-raising flour as it causes blisters to appear on the surface of the ornaments during baking. I find bread flour, sometimes referred to as "strong flour", to be the best for salt dough modelling.
>
> **Salt**
> The high salt content enables the dough to become very hard in the oven and it also prevents it from going mouldy. It is advisable to use the finest salt you can find in order for the dough to be as smooth as possible. Fine table or cooking salt is ideal.

Method of mixing
Instead of weighing out the ingredients, it is much easier to use a standard drinking beaker or mug. The ratio 2:1:1 for flour, salt and water should always be followed. If you only require a small amount of dough, measure out the ingredients to the same ratio but using a smaller container such as a tea-cup.

1 In order to avoid any unnecessary spillage, place your measuring jug or cup inside the mixing bowl.

2 Measure out the flour and salt and mix them together thoroughly.

3 Add half the water to the dry ingredients, mixing well until smooth.

4 Add the rest of the water slowly, a little at a time, until all the ingredients bind together into a pliable consistency. The dough should take in all the water easily but you may find that sometimes the dry ingredients will bind without using all the water. Above all, be careful not to add too much water. If the dough is too sticky it will take you a long time to knead in extra flour in order to bring it to the right consistency. However, if the dough is too dry and will not stick together, it is often enough to just wet your hands and carry on kneading.

5 Remove the dough from the bowl – if the right consistency has been achieved, the bowl should be free from any crumbs or deposits of flour.

TIP

It is advisable to make only one batch of dough at a time – a double quantity is very difficult to knead. If you wish to make a large ornament, make two separate batches – but always keep in mind the guidelines given on p.12 about size and the dimensions of your oven shelf!

---

6 Knead the dough for a few minutes on a dry, clean surface. When ready for modelling, it should be completely smooth and dry to touch. Note that if the dough does not hold its shape when resting on your hand this indicates that it is too wet. Alternatively, if the surface appears cracked or crumbly the dough is too dry and water should be added.

BASIC UTENSILS

Here is a list of the items required for making salt dough:

mixing bowl
measuring jug
rolling pin
pastry brush
flat-sided non-stick baking trays
ruler
flour dredger
sharp vegetable/kitchen knife
forks
modelling tools (optional)
bottle tops of different sizes
(for cutting out circles for petals of flowers)
kitchen scissors
cheese grater
garlic press
biscuit cutters or moulds
cocktail sticks and drinking straws

Cocktail Sticks are useful for making tiny holes or indentations in the dough whether you are making a lace effect on clothing, or simply enhancing decorations such as those on the harness of the rocking horse. They can also be used for making larger holes in ornaments to lace ribbon through or for hanging.

Cloves make realistic-looking stalks for fruit. Alternatively, by carefully removing the tiny ball from the clove and inserting the rest into the dough you can create the core to finish off your apple, pear or bunch of grapes. Cloves pushed right into the dough are ideal to represent an eye when making figures.

Ruler: plastic rulers can be pressed into the dough to make a quilted effect on clothing, or for making curved indentations to represent segments of a pumpkin. Make sure the ruler is clean and free from ink stains to avoid discolouring the dough.

Scissors can be used to create the effect of ears of corn. Snip into the dough as shown in the wheat sheaf.

Forks are used back to back make the woven basket effect, as shown on page 25.

Garlic Press: this is a very useful tool for making realistic-looking hair, moustaches or beards, or for the stamen of a flower. Place a small circle of dough into the crusher and press down carefully. The strands of dough which emerge should be cut off cleanly with a sharp kitchen knife.

Sharp Vegetable/Kitchen Knife: knives are mainly used for slicing measured pieces of dough and for cutting around templates, but they are also needed for making the rough bark effect on trees and veins on leaves. A special modelling tool can also be used to create the same effects.

Cheese Grater: by rolling dough gently over the grater you can get a pitted effect to make more realistic oranges or lemons.

Drinking Straws can be used for making tiny circular indentations in the dough, creating attractive patterns on clothing or decorating the centres of flowers.

Biscuit Cutters or Moulds: these are used to make the basic shapes for Christmas tree decorations or to decorate wall plaques. For biscuit cutters, roll out the dough 6 mm (¼ in) thick; for the moulds, roll out the dough 1 cm (½ in) thick. Remember to dust them with flour before pressing them into the dough to avoid distortion of the shape.

USING TEMPLATES

Some of the projects in the book are accompanied by templates to help you cut out the trickier shapes needed. Find them in the back of the book, and see below for instructions for their preparation.

1 Using tracing paper, trace the relevant templates, cut around the shape and draw it onto thin card.

2 Cut the shape out of the card and place it onto the rolled dough which has been lightly dusted with flour.

3 When cutting dough round the template, use a sawing action as opposed to pulling the knife through the dough to avoid a jagged edge.

TIPS FOR MODELLING TECHNIQUES

There are many modelling techniques described in this chapter as well as throughout the book in the different projects. But here are just a few tips which you should keep in mind before starting:

1 Use only non-stick baking trays which are either completely flat or those which have very low sides. In most cases it is a good idea to model an ornament straight onto the tray. Trays with high sides restrict your movement when rolling out and modelling dough. The only time I use a tray with high sides is for the tiny fruit and vegetables for a doll's house, as these tend to roll off flat trays! Never use old rusty trays, as the dough will stick to them.

2 To attach one part of an ornament to another, using the pastry brush wet the underside of the piece to be added. The water acts as adhesive during baking. It is not advisable to apply the water to the surface of dough onto which the piece is to go, as splashes or excess wet areas left exposed will discolour during baking and leave you with unsightly blemishes.

3 When modelling small items or parts of an ornament, put the dough which is being kept aside in a bowl covered with a damp tea-towel. This prevents the surface of the dough drying out. Make sure that the towel does not touch the dough or it will become sticky.

4 If you have finished modelling and you have some dough left, this can be saved in an airtight container or a plastic bag in a cool place (but not in the fridge). It can be kept for up to 24 hours but no longer. If kept longer it becomes too sticky to handle and no amount of kneading with flour can get it to the original smoothness. Make small figures or items for a doll's house with any leftover dough.

5 If you haven't time to finish off something you have started modelling, you can always finish off later or even the next day, even though it has started to dry. You cannot remodel the original piece, but you can add to it. Remember to use water when adding new pieces of dough.

6 When using the rolling out technique for larger items roll out directly onto your tray, and for smaller pieces roll out on a floured work surface and then transfer to the tray. Whichever is used, the surface must always be clean and free

from any sediments or grease. To ensure that the underside of your ornament is perfectly smooth and flat after baking, wipe your tray with a damp cloth before putting any dough onto it. This gives good contact keeping the ornament fixed firmly to the tray right until the ornament is ready to release itself. If the tray is too dry or has residues of grease or flour on it, the dough will not stick properly to it and the sides of your ornaments will curl up during baking.

7 When making a sausage shape, roll out the dough with the palms of your hands – fingers leave indentations.

8 When plaiting or twisting two or three strands (sausages) of dough together always start in the middle with the strands placed alongside each other. Twist or plait the first half from the middle outwards, and repeat in reverse along the other half, again working from the middle outwards. If you do not start in the centre, the strands get pulled and one end of your plait or twist will be thick while the other end will be thin.

USEFUL MODELLING TECHNIQUES

MAKING A BASKET

1 Wipe your baking tray with a damp cloth. Take a piece of dough the size of a tennis ball and, using the basket template from the back of the book as a guide, roll it out and mould it into the required shape on the lower half of your baking tray.

2 With a fork in each hand, make several rows of indentations working from top to bottom to create the basket's woven effect.

3 For the base of the basket, form a thin twist out of two pieces of dough the size of horse-chestnuts (conkers), rolled out and twisted together as above.

4 Fix the twist into position and remove any overlapping dough with the knife. Secure with a drop of water. Just above the twist, place a decorative row of small berries.

5 For the handle, take a piece of dough the size of a tennis ball and cut it in half. Form two sausage shapes 38 cm (15 in) long and 1 cm (½ in) thick, using your palms to roll the dough.

6 Twist these together carefully to form the handle and attach to the basket. Place the handle in position on the baking tray, making sure it is symmetrical and that each end adheres well to the basket – use the pastry brush and water as adhesive.

MAKING A BOW

1 With a long strip of dough, 6 mm (¼ in) thick, carefully create a bow, folding the two halves from the middle as shown.

2 Cut v-shapes out of the ribbons to give them pointed ends.

3 Cover the centre of the bow with a strip of dough measuring 1.5 cm (¾ in) wide and 5 cm (2 in) long.

TIP

Try to avoid droplets of water splashing accidentally onto the surface of your ornament – these will turn brown when the dough is baked in the oven and will look unsightly on the finished ornament.

MAKING A TWO-STRAND WREATH

1 Place the sausage shapes alongside each other, and twist them together carefully starting in the middle and working outwards along each half as shown.

2 Carefully mould the dough twist into the shape of a ring.

3 Close up the wreath by cutting the ends straight and joining them together using the pastry brush and water as adhesive.

MAKING A THREE-STRAND PLAIT

1 With three rolled out sausage shapes next to one another, begin folding into a plait starting in the middle and working outwards along one half. Repeat in reverse along the other half to complete the plait as shown in the photograph below.

2 Press the ends into a smoothed point to hide the joins at the top and bottom of the plait.

MODELLING LEAVES

1 If you require numerous leaves of a similar size, it is far quicker and easier to make a long sausage shape 1 cm (½ in) thick and cut it into 1 cm (½ in) slices. Should you require large leaves for a basket, wreath or swag, increase the diameter of the dough sausage to approximately 2.5 cm (1 in).

2 For tiny leaves, it is easier to make small balls of dough the size of peas or, for slightly larger leaves, the size of hazelnuts, press the ball to a thickness of 6 mm (¼ in) with your forefinger and proceed as below.

3 Make a point at one end by pinching the dough gently with the thumb and forefinger, and then create vein-like indentations with the knife. Making sure you don't cut right through the dough, first make one long line down the middle of the leaf and then make three or four indentations at an angle on either side of the central line.

MAKING IVY LEAVES

1 Create realistic ivy from the plain leaves described on the left by cutting out small triangles of dough from each side of the leaves as shown.

2 Gently ease out the lower part of the leaves with a knife or modelling tool, as shown below.

MAKING BERRIES

1 Take a tiny piece of dough and gently roll into a small ball between the palms of your hands.

2 Pierce each ball with the cocktail stick. The hole should not go straight through the ball, but should just appear as a deep indentation. See the berries used on various baskets for the finished effect.

MODELLING FLOWERS

Roses

1 When making roses, roll out some dough on a lightly floured surface until it is 6 mm (¼ in) thick. Using different sized bottle tops (see individual projects) cut out the necessary circles. For a large rose, four 1 cm (½ in) circles and four or five 2.5 cm (1 in) circles are used. For a smaller rose, three 6 mm (¼ in) and three or four 1 cm (½ in) circles are needed.

2 Take one of the smaller circles and fold it in half – this will represent the bud. Continue by folding (or wrapping) first the smaller petals and then the larger petals around the bud, each overlapping the last slightly, and continue until you have used up all the petals. To make the rose more realistic, pinch the upper edge of each petal with thumb and forefinger to make the petals slightly more pointed.

Primroses

1 Cut out five 1 cm (½ in) dough circles and gently pinch the top of each one to form a pointed petal shape (the size of the circles may vary in different projects). Place the five petals next to each other in a circle, each overlapping the other slightly.

2 Using the garlic press, make tiny strands of dough and place a small bunch of these together carefully in the centre of the flower to form the stamen.

3 Instead of a stamen, a tiny ball of dough decorated with a circular indentation makes a nice finishing touch. The indentation is easily made by pressing the end of a straw into the ball of dough.

Daffodils

1 Make four balls of dough the size of peas and roll each one into a small sausage shape approximately 1.5 cm (¾ in) long.

2 Press the lower halves of the sausages together to form the bell shape. Continue by flattening the upper halves which are then opened out to form the petals. Using a straw

push gently into the centre of the flower creating a circle, and finish with a stamen (see Primroses for instructions).

Violets

1 Roll out four tiny balls of dough between the palms of your hands. Flatten each one slightly and carefully pinch one side with the thumb and forefinger to form the slightly flattened petal shape.

2 Place the four petals in a circle with pointed ends together.

3 Finish off the flower with the stamen in the centre (see Primroses).

Edelweiss

1 Roll out some dough until it is 6 mm (¼ in) thick and cut out four circles for each flower using a bottle top 1.5 cm (¾ in) in diameter.

2 With each circle, fold it in half, pinch both ends slightly and push the ends together to open up the centre. The four petals give the flower its star-like appearance.

3 Place the four petals in a circle, pointed ends together, and add the stamen to the centre (see Primroses).

Apples

Roll a piece of dough into a ball and insert the end of a clove to create a stalk. You can also make a core by burying another clove (stalk first, with ball removed) into the opposite end leaving only the tip showing.

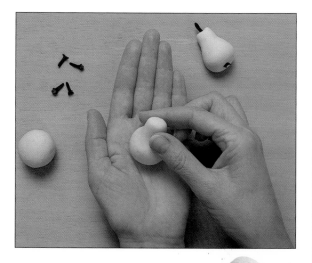

Pears

Make a smooth rounded ball of dough. Use your finger and thumb to make one half of the ball of dough slightly elongated, while keeping the other half perfectly round. Insert a clove into the top of the elongated half for the stalk.

Bananas

On a work surface, roll a ball of dough into a sausage shape with your fingers, bend it slightly in the middle to form a curved shape and make a point at each end.

Lemons

Using a piece of dough the size of a horse-chestnut, roll it into a ball and then mould pointed tips at each end. Roll the lemon gently against a cheese grater to achieve a pitted effect.

Oranges

Roll a smooth ball of dough the same size as the apple, between your hands and press it gently against the finest side of a cheese grater to achieve a realistic pitted effect. Then carefully insert a clove, stalk first, into the dough to give it the impression of the core.

Grapes

A realistic bunch of grapes can be created with lots of tiny balls of dough bunched together and piled on top of one another in a gently rounded triangular or "V" shape. Finish off the bunch with a clove at the top of the bunch to represent a stalk.

TIP

Small fruits and vegetables made for dolls' houses must be baked on a dry baking tray unlike all the other projects in this book. This is because they have to be rolled over several times during baking to ensure that no flat sides appear and that they retain their nicely rounded shapes.

Plums

These are pieces of dough rolled into a smooth oval shape with an indentation lengthways down the centre, made with a sharp knife.

BAKING

I consider baking to be the most important part. Once you have spent so much time and put so much effort into making something, it is very upsetting to ruin it during baking. It is more a process of drying out than actual baking as we understand with pastry or cakes.

If your oven is too hot, large blisters will appear on the surface, which completely spoil the appearance of wall plaques and on wreaths and larger ornaments large cracks will appear on the underside. It is advisable to bake the ornaments in the oven, either gas or electric.

You can dry them out in an airing cupboard but it is a very long process and the surface of your ornaments will be pitted, due to the slow evaporation of moisture.

Temperature

I recommend you bake your ornaments at a constant temperature of 75° C, Gas ¼ or 240° F on the middle shelf.

Cooking Times

- ornaments of ¼ in (6 mm) thickness will take up to 12 hours
- ornaments of ½ in (1 cm) thickness will take up to 18 hours
- wreaths could take up to 24-36 hours
- baskets could take up to 30-36 hours
- figures could take up to 36-48 hours

This is only a rough guide as it also depends on the overall size of the ornament as well as the thickness. Do not be impatient – it does take a long time. I actually leave the oven on overnight. You can, however, keep turning the oven off and on if you so wish. If you need to use your oven during baking, remove the ornament and keep it in a warm place, i.e. the airing cupboard, until it can be returned to the oven. If you keep it in a cold place, thereby reducing the temperature quickly, your ornament could crack.

AGA or Rayburn stoves are ideal. They have a slow oven at the bottom of the stove and although it may take the ornaments a little longer to bake, you can just leave them there until they are ready. Microwave ovens are not suitable – they are too hot!

How will you know when the ornaments are ready? When completely dry, the ornaments will automatically release themselves from the tray. If they should release themselves before they are completely dry and the underside is still soft and spongy, carry on baking until completely hard. Do not try to remove from the baking tray too soon or you will find the middle section of your ornament left behind on the tray, or even worse you will actually break your ornament.

In order to prevent cracking after baking, allow your ornaments to cool down slowly to anneal them. It is advisable to turn off your oven and allow them to cool overnight. Don't be tempted to rush this final stage.

TIP

If you are quite certain that your ornament is dry but it has not released itself from the tray, perhaps due to the fact that you are using an old tray, or you wet your tray too much during modelling, take a wooden meat tenderiser or a small hammer and give the underside of the tray a short sharp tap.

TIP

Large flat surfaces of dough should be allowed to cool down very slowly to prevent cracks. If possible leave them in the oven until completely cold.

PAINTING

Once the ornaments have been baked in the oven and are thoroughly dry and cooled, they can be painted.

When buying paints keep to the basic colours of red, yellow and blue, plus black and white. I like to have two reds, two blues, two yellows plus yellow ochre and burnt umber (for the high-baked effect). As there are so many different shades to choose from, here is a guide:

Yellow
brilliant yellow (lemon)
permanent yellow deep

Red
crimson
scarlet lake

Blue
ultramarine
Prussian blue

Plus
yellow ochre
burnt umber
black
white

TIP
If you want to make a rich red, mix both reds (crimson and scarlet lake) together; for a lovely blue mix both blues (ultramarine and Prussian blue) together.

Throughout I have used water colour brushes ranging from size 00 for the fine detail on faces to size 10 for larger areas. I find nylon brushes to be the best for painting salt dough and fortunately they tend to be the cheapest.

TIP
Water-based paints (poster paints, acrylic, gouache) are ideal for painting salt dough. Actual water-colours, however, are too insipid and will not provide a strong colour.

HIGH-BAKED EFFECT

Some of the ornaments featured in this book look as though they have been baked to a golden brown colour in the oven – they have in fact been painted (see the Fruit Wreath on p.47 for an example). You can achieve this by firstly giving your ornament a thin wash of yellow ochre. Put 1 cm (½ in) of water in a tumbler and actually mix a small amount of paint in the water. Using a paint brush, give the ornament a thin wash of this colour making sure it gets into all the cracks. The colour must be thin!

For highlighting, mix a little yellow ochre, the same amount of burnt umber and a tiny touch of scarlet on a palette or plate. Add a thin mixture of these colours to the raised areas such as the edges of leaves, petals, handles of baskets etc. and blend in with your finger so there are no hard edges.

METHOD

1 To create a thin wash of colour, add a small amount of yellow ochre paint to 1 cm (½ in) of water in a glass.

2 Using a thick brush give your ornament a thin wash of this colour, making sure you get the paint into all the folds and gaps. Remember the mixture must be quite thin and the colour weak.

3 Using a plate or a palette, make up a mixture of paint 2 parts yellow ochre, one part burnt umber and a touch of scarlet. Add a little water to mix. This colour must also be thin but is slightly darker than the ochre wash.

4 Apply a thin coat of this mixture to all raised areas on the ornament – for example, edges of leaves, petals and handles – and blend in carefully with your finger. If you wish the edges or raised areas to be just a little bit darker, add more burnt umber to the colour mix.

5 Once the paints have dried thoroughly, varnish twice on both sides. Make sure the first coat is dry before applying the second.

TIP

You might think that this high-baked effect can be achieved with egg-yolk, during baking. This, however, is not advisable. After only a few weeks the layer of egg under the varnish cracks and look unsightly.

VARNISHING

However tedious it may appear, all salt dough ornaments once baked and painted must be varnished if you want them to last. Due to the high salt content in the dough your ornaments will absorb any moisture in the atmosphere and become spongy and eventually disintegrate. I have used clear, satin finish on all the projects, although there are so many different varnishes to choose from. You could experiment with coloured varnishes – pine-coloured, oak coloured etc.

I would recommend that you give your ornaments two coats of varnish on each side. The first coat usually soaks in leaving the surface matt or patchy. Let each coat dry out thoroughly before applying the next.

MATERIALS
Tin of varnish
1 in (2.5 cm) brush
turps substitute for cleaning the brush.

REPAIRING ORNAMENTS

Salt dough once baked tends to be rather brittle. You can, however, repair damaged ornaments using a good strong, quick-acting adhesive to glue parts together. Or you can mend an ornament by moulding on a fresh piece of dough – leave it to dry out thoroughly. If the surface of the new piece after drying is slightly rough, you can always smooth it by using a piece of fine grade sandpaper. When ready, paint and varnish.

Ornaments which have been hanging on a damp wall or have been left in a damp place and have gone slightly soft, however, can be dried out again in the airing cupboard.

FINISHING OFF

Baskets and wreaths can be hung on the walls just as they are – simply balance them on a nail. However, with wall plaques and figures I have used linen tabs (poster hangers) to hang them up with. You can buy these from most craft shops for just a few pence. The tabs do actually have a self-adhesive backing but as the salt dough ornaments tend to be quite heavy, I glue these on with a strong adhesive.

To finish off the ornaments and to give the tabs extra strength, I back them with felt. Trace around the shape of the ornament or use the original template. Cut out the felt and with the use of a strong adhesive, glue the felt to the back of the ornaments – making sure there is a little extra glue between the picture tab and the felt.

STORING

Ornaments not being used, e.g. Christmas tree decorations, should be wrapped in either material or cotton wool and stored in boxes in a warm place. The airing cupboard or even the attic, which is usually warm in both summer and winter, would be suitable. Do not leave them in a damp place.

WREATHS, BASKETS AND PLAITS

Flower Basket

Decorate your home or delight one of your friends with this beautiful flower basket. Giving a feeling of abundance, this basket is decorated with a variety of flowers and leaves.

MATERIALS

1 kg (2 lbs) dough (see Tips and Techniques, p.18)

flat-sided baking tray

pastry brush

rolling pin

ruler

4 bottle tops (sizes: 6 mm (¼ in); 1 cm (½ in); 2 cm (¾ in); and 2.5 cm (1 in) in diameter)

clear, satin varnish

paint brushes

poster paints: bright colours of your choice

template (see p.00)

FOR SPECIAL EFFECTS

two forks

sharp vegetable knife

garlic press

cocktail stick

METHOD

1 Make a basket out of a piece of dough the size of a tennis ball (see Techniques, p.25).

2 Make a sausage shape 14 cm (5½ in) long and 2.5 cm (1 in) thick, and cut it into seven equal slices for the leaves. Make four normal leaves and three ivy leaves (see Tips and Techniques, p.27). Position the leaves as shown.

3 For the flowers, on a floured surface roll out a large piece of dough 6 mm (¼ in) thick.

4 To make the primrose, cut out 5 circles using the 2 cm (¾ in) bottle top and create the flower (see Tips and Techniques, p.28). Before positioning between the leaves, use a spare piece of dough to form a tiny platform for it to rest on. This prevents the flower collapsing.

5 To make the roses, for each one cut out four small circles with the 1 cm (½ in) bottle top and five larger ones with the 2 cm (¾ in) bottle top. Make two roses and position at each end of the basket (see Tips and Techniques, p.28).

6 Make three edelweiss, cutting four circles of dough for each flower using the 2 cm (¾ in) bottle top (see Tips and Techniques, p.29).

7 A tiny trickle of three violets finishes off the flower basket (see Tips and Techniques, p.29).

8 Any gaps are filled with leaves made from hazelnut-sized pieces of dough (see Tips and Techniques, p.27). When complete, bake the basket referring to the instructions on p.32.

9 Once baked, the basket can be painted with brightly coloured poster paints, and when these are thoroughly dry, it should be varnished twice on both sides.

Fruit Basket

Celebrate harvest festivities with this lovely wall decoration. Made with wholemeal flour, this basket has a rustic appearance and is decorated with plump harvest fruits.

MATERIALS

1 kg (2 lbs) of wholemeal dough
(see Tips and Techniques, p.18)
flat-sided baking tray
rolling pin
pastry brush
ruler
1 bottle top (size: 2 cm (¾ in) in diameter)
poster paints: yellow ochre, green, purple, red
paint brushes
clear, satin varnish

FOR SPECIAL EFFECTS

two forks
sharp vegetable knife
cocktail stick
1 straw
cloves

METHOD

1 Make a basket in exactly the same way as the Flower Basket (see Tips and Techniques, p.25 and p.38).

2 To create the arrangement start with the leaves. Form a sausage shape 7.5 cm (3 in) long and 2.5 cm (1 in) thick, and cut it into 6 equal slices.

3 Keeping one of the slices aside, make five large leaves with the remaining ones, (see Tips and Techniques, p.27). Place them onto the basket making sure they adhere well – two at the top and three arranged half way down the basket, as shown.

4 Cut the leftover slice of dough in half, roll the two pieces into balls and make two

smaller leaves to be placed at the sides of the basket, between the larger leaves.

5 Roll out some dough on a floured work surface to a thickness of 6 mm (¼ in), and cut out 10 circles with the bottle top. Use these pieces to create two primroses (see Tips and Techniques, p.28), and position the flowers near the smaller leaves.

6 The apple, plum and pear are made from 3 pieces of dough the size of horse-chestnuts (conkers), (see Tips and Techniques, p.30).

7 Finish off with a small bunch of grapes (see Tips and Techniques, p31).

8 Fill remaining gaps with small leaves (see Tips and Techniques, p.27).

9 Using the instructions on p.32, bake the basket in the oven.

10 After baking, give the basket a very thin wash with yellow ochre, the leaves a thin wash of green, the grapes a wash of purple and the flowers a wash of red.

11 Once thoroughly dry, the basket should be varnished with a clear, satin varnish – two coats on each side.

VARIATION

This basket can be made with white bread flour (see Tips and Techniques, p18) and after baking given a thin wash of yellow ochre. The raised areas can then be highlighted using a high-baked effect (see Tips and Techniques, p.34).

Apple Wreath

This simple wreath is very effective when decorated with rosy red apples. A hint of sophistication is added with a bow made out of dough and painted in a contrasting colour.

MATERIALS

1 kg (2 lbs) dough (see Tips and Techniques, p.18)
rolling pin
flat-sided baking tray
pastry brush
ruler
sharp vegetable knife
clove
poster paints: red, dark green
paint brushes
clear, satin varnish

METHOD

1 Using half the dough, make a sausage shape 56 cm (22 in) long and 2.5 cm (1 in) thick. Wipe the baking tray with a damp cloth, place the sausage onto it in the shape of a ring. Join the ends together neatly (see Tips and Techniques, p.26).

2 Flatten the surface of the wreath slightly with a rolling pin to create an even platform for the apples.

3 Using half of the remaining dough, make a sausage 14 cm (5½ in) long and 2.5 cm (1 in) thick. Cut it into seven equal slices for the seven apples (see Tips and Techniques, p.30).

4 Make eight leaves out of a sausage shape of dough 10 cm (4 in) long and 1 cm (½ in) thick. Cut into eight equal slices (see Tips and Techniques, p.27).

5 Before placing the apples and leaves onto the dough, plan carefully where they are to be positioned. Try to create a symmetrical look, leaving enough room at the bottom for the pastry bow. Position two leaves at the top and three down each side and rest one apple on the tip of each leaf.

6 Roll out the remaining dough and create a decorative bow out of a strip 41 cm (16 in) long and 4.5 cm (1¼ in) wide (see Tips and Techniques, p.26).

7 The bow should nestle between two apples, but not cover them at all. Make sure it adheres well to the wreath, with the ribbons flowing onto the tray.

8 Bake your wreath referring to the instructions on p.32.

9 The wreath itself should be left natural in colour. Only the apples and leaves are painted in bright colours, and the bow is painted a rich dark green.

10 Once the paints have dried thoroughly, the wreath should be given two coats of varnish on each side.

VARIATION

As an alternative, a variety of different fruits such as pears, plums or oranges could be arranged around this wreath. For a completely different look, instead of baking in bright colours, the wreath could be given a high-baked effect.

Flower Plait

Three-strand plaits are an attractive alternative to wreaths. This plait has been decorated with leaves and roses, but you could also use various fruits.

MATERIALS

1 kg (2 lbs) dough (see Tips and Techniques, p.18)

flat-sided baking tray

rolling pin

pastry brush

ruler

sharp vegetable knife

2 bottle tops (sizes: 1 cm (½ in) and 2 cm (¾ in) in diameter)

cocktail stick

poster paints: yellow ochre, dark red, green

paint brushes

clear, satin varnish

METHOD

1 Using two-thirds of the dough, make three sausage shapes 1 cm (½ in) thick and 38 cm (15 in) long.

2 Use these to form the plait, (see Tips and Techniques, p.26). Press the ends together to form points. When complete, the plait should be approximately 25.5 cm (10 in) long, and 7.5 cm (3 in) wide in the middle.

3 Wipe the baking tray with a damp cloth and carefully transfer the plait onto it.

4 Using a cocktail stick, make a large hole straight through the top of the plait. This hole will be used to thread the ribbon through after baking.

5 Roll out some dough until it is 6 mm (¼ in) thick, and for each rose cut out 2 small and 4 large circles using the two bottle tops. Make two roses, one for each end of the plait, (see Tips and Techniques, p.28).

6 With four pieces of dough the size of hazelnuts, make the leaves and position one on either side of each rose (see Tips and Techniques, p.27).

7 To finish off, decorate the folds of the plait with berries (see Tips and Techniques, p.27). You can also add a little touch by creating a decorative necklace of berries to go behind each rose (see photograph).

8 Bake the plait referring to the instructions on p.32.

9 Once the ornament is thoroughly dry, paint the plait in a yellow ochre wash (refer to Tips and Techniques, p.33). The roses should be painted a dark red and the leaves a bright green. Finally, varnish twice on both sides, allowing the plait to dry thoroughly between coats. Thread a length of ribbon through the hole.

Fruit Wreath

Decorated with fruit, this high-baked wreath has a very wholesome appearance and makes a perfect wall hanging for harvest time. If you wish, paint the fruits their proper colours for a more realistic look.

MATERIALS

1 kg (2 lbs) dough (see Tips and Techniques, p.18)
flat-sided baking tray
rolling pin
pastry brush
ruler
sharp vegetable knife
cloves
poster paints: yellow ochre, burnt umber, scarlet
paint brushes
clear, satin varnish

METHOD

1 Using three-quarters of the dough, make two sausage shapes 46 cm(18 in) long and 2.5 cm (1 in) thick.

2 Twist these together to make the wreath (see Tips and Techniques, p.26). After wiping your tray with a damp cloth, carefully transfer the wreath onto it.

3 With the remaining dough, make a sausage shape 5 cm (2 in) long and 2.5 cm (1 in) thick. Cut it into five equal slices and make the leaves (see Tips and Techniques, p.27).

4 Place the leaves on the lower part of the wreath over the join.

5 Finish the arrangement with two apples and one pear (see Tips and Techniques, p.30)

6 Once the fruit and leaves are all fixed in position, fill any gaps with bunches of berries (see Tips and Techniques, p.27), to create a look of abundance.

7 Bake the wreath referring to the instructions on p.32.

8 When thoroughly dry, give the wreath and the fruit a thin wash of yellow ochre all over and paint the raised areas with a mixture of yellow ochre, burnt umber and scarlet to create a high-baked effect (see Tips and Techniques, p.34). Once the paints have dried thoroughly, carefully varnish the wreath twice on both sides.

Heart-shaped Plait

This beautiful plaited heart has been decorated with roses and leaves and would make a lovely gift for Mother's Day or Valentine's Day.

MATERIALS

1 kg (2 lbs) dough (see Tips and Techniques, p.18)
flat-sided baking tray
rolling pin
pastry brush
ruler
sharp vegetable knife
2 bottle tops (sizes: 1 cm (½ in) and 2 cm (¾ in) in diameter)
cocktail stick
poster paints: yellow ochre, burnt umber, scarlet
clear, satin varnish
ribbon, 31 cm (12 in) long and 1 cm (½ in) wide

METHOD

1 The heart is made in two separate halves. For each half make 3 sausage shapes 48 cm (19 in) long and ½ in (1 cm) thick.

2 To make one half, plait the strands together (see Tips and Techniques, p.26). Wipe your tray with a damp cloth and place the plait onto it in the shape of half the heart. Repeat this step for the other half.

3 Fix the two halves of the heart securely together, pinching the joins top and bottom to form points.

4 Make six leaves from a sausage shape 6 cm (2 in) long and 1 cm (½ in) thick, cut into six equal slices (see Tips and Techniques, p.27). Place three at the top and three at the bottom as shown, leaving a space in the middle of them for the roses.

5 Using a piece of dough rolled out to 6 mm (¼ in) thick, cut out 8 small and 8 large circles using the bottle tops to make the two roses (see Tips and Techniques, p.28).

6 Place one rose at the base and one on the centre point of the heart, and make little berries to finish off the decoration (see Tips and Techniques, p.27).

7 Before baking, make two large holes at the top of each half of the heart with the cocktail stick.

8 Bake the heart referring to the instructions on p.32.

9 Once baked and cooled, the heart can be given a thin colour wash in yellow ochre and the leaves, flowers and tiny balls of dough given a high-baked effect (see Tips and Techniques, p.34). When the paints are dry, varnish twice on both sides, allowing it to dry thoroughly between coats.

10 When the varnish is thoroughly dry, thread the ribbon through the holes and tie a knot in the ends.

Two-strand Wreath with Bow and Flowers

This otherwise chunky wreath is given a delicate appearance when decorated with pretty flowers and a pastry bow. After varnishing, the edges of the ribbon have been painted with a gold-coloured felt-tip pen.

MATERIALS

1 kg (2 lbs) dough (see Tips and Techniques, p.18)
flat-sided baking tray
rolling pin
pastry brush
ruler
sharp vegetable knife
2 bottle tops (sizes: 1 cm (½ in) and 2 cm (¾ in) in diameter)
garlic press
poster paints: bright colours of your choice
paint brushes
clear, satin varnish
gold-coloured felt tip pen

METHOD

1 Using two-thirds of the dough, make two sausage shapes 38 cm (15 in) long and 2.5 cm (1 in) in diameter.

2 Make your wreath (see Tips and Techniques, p.26), and transfer it carefully onto the baking tray. Remember to wipe the tray first with a damp cloth.

3 Make a pastry bow out of a strip 41 cm (16 in) long and 4 cm (1¾ in) wide (see Tips and Techniques, p.26).

4 Before placing the bow onto your wreath, flatten the area where the bow will be placed with your fingers, to form a platform. It should be placed over the join of the wreath, letting the ribbons flow onto the baking tray.

5 Gather up any leftover dough and knead it again until smooth in order to use it for the flowers and leaves.

6 Make three small leaves out of a sausage shape 3 cm (1¼ in) long and 1 cm (½ in) thick, cut into three equal slices (see Tips and Techniques, p.27).

7 Place the leaves onto the top of the wreath, opposite the bow (see photograph).

8 Roll out the leftover dough until 6 mm (¼ in) thick, and cut out 4 small and 5 large circles using the bottle tops. Make the rose (see Tips and Techniques, p.28), and nestle it between the leaves.

9 Out of the remaining dough, make 12 tiny balls of dough and create three little violets to complete the decorations (see Tips and Techniques, p.29). Position as shown in the photograph opposite.

10 Bake the wreath referring to the instructions on p.32.

11 The wreath should be left natural in colour. Only the flowers, leaves and bow should be painted in bright colours of your choice, and once dry, two coats of varnish should be applied to both sides. When the varnish has thoroughly dried, the upper edges of the bow can be carefully highlighted with the gold felt tip pen.

CHILD'S PLAY

Alice

Alice makes a lovely wall decoration for a child's room, recalling the magic of her adventures in Wonderland. Use paints in the colours shown here to create a traditional-style Alice. Don't forget her striped stockings!

MATERIALS

1 kg (2 lbs) dough (see Tips and Techniques, p.18)

flat-sided baking tray

rolling pin

pastry brush

ruler

sharp vegetable knife

cocktail stick

tracing paper

thin card and scissors

poster paints: bright colours of your choice

paint brushes

clear, satin varnish

linen tab

felt

PREPARATION

Prepare the Alice templates from the back of the book – her body, apron, sleeves, skirt, frills, and hair (for method see Tips and Techniques, p.24).

METHOD

1 After wiping your baking tray with a damp cloth, roll out half the dough directly onto your tray until it is 1 cm (½ in) thick, making sure you leave at least 7.5 cm (3 in) of space at the top of the tray.

2 Dust the surface of the dough with a little flour and place the template of Alice's body onto it. With the knife cut around it carefully (see Tips and Techniques, p.24). Remove any excess dough.

3 It is important to soften all the outlines of the body by patting the dough carefully with your forefinger. With the knife, tuck the edges touching the tray under the body to complete the soft rounded appearance and to avoid any hard edges.

4 For Alice's head, form a ball of dough the size of a horse-chestnut (conker) and press it securely onto the shoulders.

5 Make a deep vertical indentation down the centre of the legs, but do not cut right through the dough.

6 Roll out some dough until it is 6 mm (¼ in) thick, and with the help of the templates, cut out the skirt, dress, and sleeves (see Tips and Techniques, p.24).

7 Wet the lower half of Alice's body with the pastry brush and water, and carefully place the skirt over the body and legs. Give the skirt some soft folds.

11 Cut out strips of dough 8 cm long (3 in) long and 6 mm (¼ in) wide, and create two frills down the sides of the bodice. Make a tiny frill for Alice's neck.

12 With a thin strip of dough, make a belt for Alice's dress. Before adding the sleeves gather the upper and lower edges, as shown. Thin strips of dough form the cuffs.

13 Using the template, cut the hair shape from a piece of dough 6 mm (¼ in) thick. Make several straight indentations with the knife to create strands of hair, then attach the hair-piece over the top of the head so that it rests on the tray at the back and sides. Finish off with a hair band placed on top of the hair.

8 Stick the bodice of the apron onto Alice, tucking the straps over her shoulders. If the straps are too long, cut off the excess with the knife. Add the apron skirt. Give the bodice and skirt a lacy effect with a cocktail stick.

9 Make oval pieces of dough for the feet and position at the bottom of the legs at an angle. Cover the join with strips for shoe straps.

10 The arms are made with sausage shapes 8.5 cm (3¼ in) long and tapering from 1 cm (½ in) thick at the shoulder to 6 mm (¼ in) at the wrist. The hands are two small ovals which are attached to the arms once the arms are in place. Score fingers with a knife.

14 Bake Alice referring to the instructions on p.32. When thoroughly dry, Alice can be painted. When painting the face, keep the natural colour of the dough for her complexion, and use a very thin brush for the eyes and mouth. With the tip of your finger, blend in a bit of red on the cheeks. Once the paints are dry varnish twice on both sides.

15 When the ornament is completely finished and dry, fix on a linen tab and cover Alice's back, including the tab, with felt (see Tips and Techniques, p.35).

Rocking Horse

This is a lovely colourful wall decoration for a child's bedroom and, with the use of the template, is really easy to make.

MATERIALS

1 kg (2 lbs) dough (see Tips and Techniques, p.18)
flat-sided baking tray
pastry brush
rolling pin
ruler
garlic press
cocktail stick
tracing paper
thin card and scissors
poster paints: yellow ochre and
bright colours of your choice
paint brushes
clear, satin varnish

PREPARATION

Prepare the Rocking Horse templates from the back of the book (for method see Tips and Techniques, p.24).

METHOD

1 Wipe the baking tray with a damp cloth and roll out all the dough directly onto your baking tray to a thickness of 1 cm (½ in).

2 Using the Rocking Horse template, cut out the shape and remove any excess dough (see Tips and Techniques, p.24).

3 Soften the outlines with your forefinger and, with the knife, tuck any sharp edges on the tray underneath to complete the softly rounded appearance.

4 With a spare piece of dough, create a small flat platform to rest the tail on so that it is on the same level as the rest of the shape.

5 Using the garlic press make long, thin strands of dough for the mane and tail. Fix them carefully into place.

6 Gather up any leftover pieces of dough and, on a floured surface, roll it to a thickness of 6 mm (¼ in). With the template, cut out the saddle and place it on the horse, folding it over its back and using water to make sure it adheres.

7 Form the facial harness and the saddle harness with strips of dough 1 cm (½ in) thick and place in position.

8 A thin strip of dough is placed on the saddle to represent the raised edge of the blanket.

9 Cut out two little pieces of dough in the shape of hooves. Place at the bottom of the legs, just above the rocker.

10 The rocker, saddle and harness are all decorated with little pieces of dough in the same shape as berries (see Tips and Techniques, p.27).

11 Bake the rocking horse referring to the instructions on p.32.

12 Once dry, give the ornament a thin yellow ochre wash (see Tips and Techniques, p.33), and paint with bright colours as shown in the photograph on p.59. When the paint is thoroughly dry, varnish twice on both sides with satin varnish, leaving the horse to dry between coats.

Rocking Horse and Teddy Bear Plaques

I was once lucky enough to find these beautiful biscuit moulds – a teddy and a rocking horse. They enabled me to make this pretty wall decoration for a child. However, any type of mould would do, and it is amazing what you can find amongst your children's toys as well. In the method, substitute other characters from your own moulds.

MATERIALS

1 kg (2 lb) dough (see Tips and Techniques, p.18)
flat-sided baking tray
ruler
rolling pin
sharp vegetable knife
your choice of biscuit moulds
cocktail stick
poster paints: your choice of colours
paint brushes
clear, satin varnish
ribbon 1 cm (½ in) wide, length as required

METHOD

1 Roll out your dough on a floured work-surface until it is 1 cm (½ in) thick.

2 Plan carefully where to press the moulds into the soft dough, and sprinkle that surface with a little flour. Press the moulds down into the dough, making sure you do not twist the mould and alter the shape as you do so, then remove the mould.

3 With the help of a ruler decide the shape and size of your plaque. Leaving a gap of 1 cm (½ in) around the indentations of the mould, cut away the excess dough using a sharp knife. You may find it easier to create a rough paper template for your plaque to help guide you when you are cutting it out of the rolled dough and to ensure that you leave a sufficiently wide border.

4 Wipe the tray with a damp cloth and transfer the plaque carefully to the tray.

5 Before placing in the oven, make four holes through the dough with a cocktail stick – two at the top and two at the bottom. Make the holes quite large – they tend to close up slightly during baking.

6 Bake the plaque referring to the instructions on p.32.

7 Finally, paint your plaque in bright colours, and once these are thoroughly dry, finish off with two coats of varnish on each side.

8 Thread ribbon through the holes for hanging, or simply as decoration.

Bread, Fruit and Vegetables for a Doll's House

After modelling a larger item, you will probably have some dough left over and don't quite know what to do with it. Salt dough doesn't keep very well and after 24 hours will have to be thrown away. The ideal way to use it up is to make small items for a doll's house.

MATERIALS

leftover salt dough
baking tray with high sides
sharp vegetable knife
pastry brush
cocktail knife
cheese grater
poster paints: yellow ochre, burnt umber and scarlet
for bread, as required for fruit and vegetables
paint brushes
clear, satin varnish

METHOD

Before you start, give your baking tray a good wipe with a damp cloth. You should chose the dimensions of the various doll's house decorations yourself, based on the size of the house they are required for.

Bread

There are many different types of loaves and rolls and here I have chosen a selection of the more traditional varieties.

1 For a cottage loaf make two balls of dough in slightly different sizes. Place the larger ball at the bottom and the smaller ball at the top and

---

TIP

Make sure the bread loaves really sticks to the tray by pressing them securely on before baking. Otherwise the loaves will not have flat bottoms!

---

ensure they adhere. Make a hole in the top with a cocktail stick.

2 An ordinary loaf can be made by moulding into shape a piece of dough the size of a small horse-chestnut (conker) with the thumb and forefinger of both hands.

3 For the French Stick, make a thin sausage of dough pointed at each end, and with a knife create diagonal indentations along its length.

4 Baps (bread rolls) are little round balls of dough flattened slightly.

5 The bread loaves will take approximately four to five hours to bake (see p.32).

6 When thoroughly dry they should be painted with a thin wash of yellow ochre and then given a high-baked effect along their tops (see Tips and Techniques, p.34)

Fruit

1 There is really no limit to the variety of fruit you can make using salt dough. For miniature fruit, use tiny pea-sized balls of dough and follow the instructions to make apples, bananas, pears, plums, oranges, lemons and grapes (see Tips and Techniques, p.30).

2 It should only take a couple of hours for the fruit to bake (see p.32). After baking, paint the fruit in as realistic colours as possible, and when dry, varnish twice on both sides.

Vegetables

1 Potatoes are the easiest to make. Make tiny balls of dough, slightly irregular in shape.

2 Cauliflowers and cabbages are little balls of dough with flat circles of dough wrapped around, each overlapping the other, for the leaves. Prick the centre of the cauliflower with a cocktail stick. Leave the cabbage centre smooth.

3 Carrots are tiny sausages of dough with one end cut straight and the other end pointed. Round off straight ends to make them realistic.

4 Bake the vegetables, referring to the instructions on p.32 if necessary.

5 Finally, paint the vegetables in colours of your choice or with a thin yellow ochre wash for an earthy look. When the paints are dry, varnish twice on both sides.

There are so many other items you can make like bottles of milk, pies, hams, joints of beef, fish, cakes etc. If your items need to stand up, make sure the base is straight by placing them on a wet tray before baking.

Father Christmas

This chubby Father Christmas makes a colourful wall decoration at Christmas time. Try to make him as plump as possible.

MATERIALS

1 kg (2 lbs) dough (see Tips and Techniques, p.18)
pastry brush
rolling pin
ruler
sharp vegetable knife
garlic press
tracing paper
thin card and scissors
poster paints: bright colours of your choice
paint brushes
clear, satin varnish

PREPARATION

Prepare Father Christmas' cloak and hat templates at the back of the book (for method see Tips and Techniques, p.24).

METHOD

1 Wipe the baking tray with a damp cloth. Using a piece of dough the size of a horse-chestnut (conker), mould the head and position it directly on the tray 5 cm (2 in) from the top. Make a plump nose with a ball of dough.

2 The body should be quite plump. For this, use a piece of dough the size of a tennis ball slightly flattened, placed directly under the head.

3 The legs/trousers are sausage shapes 6 cm (2¼ in) long, and 3 cm (1¼ in) thick. Attach each one securely to lower edge of the body.

4 Model the boots out of two balls of dough the size of horse-chestnuts and attach them to the end of the legs. Make indentations with the knife underneath the boots for the heels.

5 Roll the rest of the dough until it is 6 mm (¼ in), and dust with flour. Cut around the template for one side of the jacket. Repeat for the other side. Wet the body and lay the jacket onto it, making sure it touches the tray.

6 Edge the boots and the jacket with strips of dough 6 mm (¼ in) thick. Give a fur-like effect with the help of a cocktail stick.

7 For the belt, use a narrow strip of dough and a square of dough for the buckle.

8 Tiny strands or strips of dough can be placed around the head for hair. Remember most of the head will be covered with the hat so only strands around the face are necessary.

9 Father Christmas just wouldn't be complete without his long flowing beard. Use the garlic press to make several very thin strands of dough, bunch them together in the shape of a beard, and secure under the face. Mould a moustache to finish off. After placing in position, make a hole with a cocktail stick or modelling tool between the moustache and beard for his mouth.

10 For the hat, roll out some dough until it is 1 cm (½ in) thick, dust it with flour and cut the shape out using the template. Fix the hat all the way round the head from the shoulders, tucking it under the edges of the head carefully and making sure it touches the tray. Add a bobble and some fur!

11 The arms are made from sausage shapes 11.5 cm (4½ in) long, tapering in thickness from 1.5 cm (1 in) at the cuff to 1 cm (½ in) at the shoulder. The arms should be fixed to the body so that one arm is bent completely

at the elbow up to the shoulder, and the other bent inwards to rest on his chest. Finish off the cuffs with some fur.

12 The hands are made of two oval-shaped pieces of dough with indentations for the fingers and thumbs. Fix them securely to the end of the arms – one on the chest, the other over the shoulder where it will hold the bag.

13 Out of any remaining dough make a sack from a piece of dough the size of a horse-chestnut (conker). Give the impression of gathered material. The little doll held in his arms is made of small balls of dough for the head and body; the garlic press is used for her hair.

14 Father Christmas will take about 3 days to bake, refer to the instructions on p32.

15 Once baked paint the figure in bright Christmas colours – you can add imaginative detail to all the features. Finally, when the paints have dried, varnish twice on both sides.

Girl in Pink

Salt dough really lends itself to making figures. The plumper they are the better they look. Forget all you have ever learned about proportioning, and have a go at creating this figure. The little boy is made in exactly the same way.

MATERIALS

1 kg (2 lbs) dough (see Tips and Techniques, p.18)
flat-sided baking tray
rolling pin
ruler
pastry brush
sharp vegetable knife
plastic ruler
cocktail stick
poster paints: your choice of bright colours
paint brushes
clear, satin varnish

METHOD

1 Wipe the baking tray with a damp cloth. Using a piece of dough the size of a tennis ball, make a sausage shape 15 cm (6 in) long and 5 cm (2 in) thick. Place this directly onto your baking tray and flatten slightly. At the top end, taper both sides to form shoulders.

2 Mould the head out of a ball of dough the size of a horse-chestnut (conker), and attach it to the shoulders making sure it adheres well.

3 To form the legs, starting from the bottom of the sausage shape cut straight through the dough to half way up the body. Ease the legs apart slightly with the knife. Try to make the legs a little less angular by modelling them into shape with your fingers. Make two indentations in each knee with a cocktail stick for dimples.

4 With the use of the plastic ruler, make a quilted effect on the upper body (see Tips and Techniques p.22).

5 For the top of the boots, roll out a flat piece dough until it is 6 mm (¼ in) thick, and cut two strips 6 cm (2½ in) wide and 1.5 cm (¾ in) long. Cover the shins with the strips folding round the leg and tucking the dough underneath at the sides.

6 Using oval-shaped pieces of dough make the two feet and add an indentation two-thirds of the way along them to suggest the heel. Stick these securely to the legs making sure the shoe and leg parts of the boots now blend into one all the way round.

7 The pleated skirt is made from a long strip of dough 25 cm (10 in) long, 5 cm (2 in) wide and 6 mm (¼ in) thick, folded as shown. Fix the skirt onto the figure and making sure it touches the tray at either side.

8 Place thin strips of dough, one around the neck and one across the waist, to represent the cardigan rib – try making little vertical indentations along the strips to achieve the ribbed effect.

9 Add a few buttons down the front of the cardigan, using tiny balls of dough flattened slightly. Make two holes in each button with the cocktail stick.

10 Make a sausage 18 cm (7 in) and 1.5 cm (¾ in) thick, and cut it in half and use as two arms. Place the arms carefully onto the body, curving them slightly so her hands rest on the skirt, and mould the shape of the shoulders at the top. Taper the end of each arm to form the cuffs of the cardigan and decorate as above.

11 The hands are oval shaped pieces of dough with indentations for fingers and thumbs. Make sure they stick to both the arms and the skirt.

12 The hair is made up of two plaits. Using a ball of dough the size of a horse-chestnut (conker) and divided into three pieces, make three sausage shapes 6 mm (¼ in) thick and create one long plait (see Tips and Techniques, p.26). Cut it in half and fix the plaits to the sides of the head, letting them fall in front of the shoulders. The fringe is made from strands of dough which have been forced through the garlic press. Add two tiny bows to the plaits.

13 To finish off the figure add a beret made from a ball of dough the size of a horse-chestnut (conker), flattened into the right shape and folded around the top of the head and hair. It should touch the tray at the back. The beret is decorated with tiny indentations along the front edge, and a little bobble on top!

14 This figure will take 3 days to dry out thoroughly. Bake referring to the instructions on p.32.

15 When thoroughly dry, the figure can be painted in bright colours of your choice – perhaps colour co-ordinated with the room where she will hang. When painting the face, keep the natural colour of the dough for her complexion, and use a very thin brush for the eyes and mouth. With the tip of your finger, blend in a bit of red on the cheeks, and once the paints are dry varnish twice on both sides.

16 If you would like to make a partner for this little girl, try making the boy to match. He has been made in exactly the same way, but given trousers instead of a skirt.

Cock and Hen

With the use of the templates, these birds are very easy to make and when hanging on the wall face to face they can look really effective.

MATERIALS

1 kg (2 lbs) dough (see Tips and Techniques, p.18)
flat-sided baking tray
rolling pin
ruler
sharp vegetable knife
cocktail stick
pastry brush
cloves
thin card and scissors
tracing paper
poster paints: yellow ochre, burnt umber, scarlet
paint brushes
clear, satin varnish
linen tabs
felt

PREPARATION

Prepare the cock and hen templates from the back of the book (for method see Tips and Techniques, p.24).

METHOD

1 On a lightly floured surface, roll out all the dough until it is 1 cm (½ in) thick.

2 Dust the dough lightly with flour and place the templates onto it. Cut round each template carefully, pull away the excess dough, and tidy edges of each shape.

3 Wipe the baking tray with a damp cloth and transfer the birds onto it carefully.

4 Make seventeen balls of dough the size of hazelnuts. Stick five of these onto the tail of the hen and use the rest to create the plumage of the cock. Decorate them with cloves.

5 Small oblong-shaped pieces of dough, 1 cm (½ in) thick, are placed on the tops of their heads and larger oblongs form the platforms at the bottom. Using a sharp vegetable knife make indentations vertically in their "crowns" and put holes into the platforms at the bottom with a cocktail stick.

6 Both birds are decorated with little rows of berry-shaped pieces of dough (see Tips and Techniques, p.27). Use the photograph of the finished birds as a guide.

7 Use cloves for the eyes, making sure they are fixed securely in position.

8 Baking will take about 18 hours – refer to the instructions on p.32.

9 When thoroughly dried, paint the birds with a thin colour wash of yellow ochre, and then give the plumage, crowns, bases and decorations a high-baked effect (see Tips and Techniques, p.34). Once the paints are dry, varnish the birds twice on both sides.

10 To hang the cock and hen, fix small linen tabs, glued on with a strong adhesive, onto their backs. Finish off with a layer of felt (see Tips and Techniques, p.35).

SPECIAL OCCASIONS

Easter Wreath

Make this lovely table decoration at Easter time and fill it with either painted or chocolate eggs – the children will love it!

MATERIALS

2 kg (4 lbs) dough (see Tips and Techniques, p.18)
flat-sided baking tray
pastry brush
rolling pin
1 egg
rabbit-shaped biscuit mould
poster paints: yellow ochre, burnt umber, scarlet
paint brushes
clear, satin varnish

METHOD

1 Using three-quarters of the dough (1.5 kg/ 3 lbs), make two sausage shapes 72 cm (28½ in) long, and 2.5 cm (1 in) thick.

2 To create the wreath, twist the two strands together and form into a circle (see Tips and Techniques, p.26).

3 Wipe over the baking tray with a clean, damp cloth and then transfer the wreath carefully onto it.

4 Using the egg sideways, press it into the soft dough to form indentations in five places at regular intervals along the wreath. Do not press down too hard, the egg should not go through to the tray.

5 Roll out the remaining dough until it is 1 cm (½ in) thick. Using the biscuit cutter, cut out ten rabbit shapes. Add to each cut-out a tiny ball of dough to emphasize the tail, and a small sausage shape to accentuate the ear.

6 Stick the rabbits securely to the wreath, one at each side of the egg-shaped indentation. They should stick to the side of the wreath with their feet touching the tray.

7 Bake the wreath referring to the instructions on p.32.

8 Paint the wreath with a yellow ochre colour wash, and then highlight the raised areas with a high-baked effect (see Tips and Techniques, p.34). Finally when the paints are dry, varnish twice on both sides. I prefer to use a clear, satin varnish but you can experiment with gloss varnish or even pine-coloured varnish.

Easter Egg Lady

This delightful peasant-style egg lady makes a lovely wall decoration all year round. She has been made to look really plump and rounded, and carries two dough eggs to remind us of Easter festivities.

MATERIALS

1 kg (2 lbs) dough (see Tips and Techniques, p.18)
flat-sided baking tray
rolling pin
pastry brush
1 egg
cocktail stick
sharp vegetable knife
tracing paper
thin card
scissors
poster paints: yellow ochre, burnt sienna and scarlet
paint brushes
clear, satin varnish

PREPARATION

Prepare the apron and the bodice templates from the back of the book (for method, see Tips and Techniques, p.24).

METHOD

1 Wipe the baking tray over with a clean damp cloth.

2 For the head, form a neatly rounded ball of dough the size of a medium-sized tomato. Place this onto the tray about 5 cm (2 in) from the top.

3 The upper body is formed of a piece of dough the size of a large apple. It should be large enough to fit in both hands when cupped together. Pat this dough into an oval shape 12 cm (5 in) wide, 9 cm (3½ in) long, and 1.5 cm (½ in) thick, and place it below the head to form the upper body, shoulders and arms.

4 Using a piece of dough the same size again, pat this into the shape of the lower body/skirt, allowing the waist to overlap the upper body slightly. Make sure the two halves of the body are stuck together securely.

5 Using the egg, press down into the soft dough at each side of her upper body. The arms are pressed out slightly and at least 1.5 cm (½ in) should be showing around the egg. Remove the egg as it is only used to make the indentation.

6 For the "bosom", use two hazelnut-sized pieces of dough rolled into balls and place on her chest.

7 Roll out the remaining dough until it is 6 mm (¼ in) thick, and cut out the apron bodice and apron using the templates. Add a rounded circle of dough for her stomach, before positioning the apron on top.

8 Make sure the two pieces of clothing adhere well to the body, and finally add a thin strip of dough for the waistband.

9 Make a necklace out of a ring of tiny balls of dough, leaving room for the straps of the apron to fit either side of it.

10 Using a cocktail stick, make a lace-effect around the neckline of the bodice and around the edge of the apron.

11 Small balls of dough, the same shape as berries (see Tips and Techniques, p.27), decorate the apron.

12 Two long strips of dough finish off the base of the skirt.

13 For the hair, make two small plaits from a sausage shape 6 mm (¼ in) thick, plaited and cut in half (see Tips and Techniques, p.26). At the ends of each plait, create strands of hair using the knife and finish off with small strips of dough for ribbons. Place the plaits onto the head, allowing them to fall over the shoulders.

14 The hat is made from a ball of dough the size of a hazelnut and patted into shape. Cover the plait at the front and make three holes in the hat with a cocktail stick.

15 The features of the face are indentations made using the cocktail stick.

16 Finally, the eggs can be moulded out of the remaining dough. Wet the hollows under both arms with your pastry brush and water, and drop the eggs into them carefully.

17 Bake the figure referring to the instructions on p.32.

18 Once the egg-lady is dry, use a colour wash of yellow ochre to paint the figure and then apply the high-baked effect to all raised areas. Finally, varnish twice on both sides.

Wheat Sheaf

Harvest festival would not be complete without this wholesome wheat sheaf. Given a high-baked effect with poster paints, this wall decoration looks lovely all year round.

MATERIALS

1 kg (2 lbs) dough (see Tips and Techniques, p.18)
low-sided baking tray
pastry brush
rolling pin
ruler
sharp vegetable knife
scissors
tracing paper
thin card
poster paints: yellow ochre, burnt umber, scarlet
paint brushes
clear, satin varnish
linen tab
strong adhesive
felt

PREPARATION

Prepare the Wheat Sheaf template from the back of the book (for method, see Tips and Techniques, p.24).

METHOD

1 Wipe the tray with a damp cloth and roll out half the dough until it is 6 mm (¼ in) thick directly onto the tray.

2 Dust the dough lightly with flour, then place the template onto it and cut round with the knife (see Tips and Techniques, p.24). Pull away any excess dough.

3 Remove the template and using the pastry brush wet the surface of the dough slightly.

4 Roll out several long very thin strips for stalks. Stick them close together, on the trunk of the wheat sheaf.

5 Make the last three strips into a thin plait (see Tips and Techniques, p.26), and strap it round the narrow part of the wreath.

6 Using three-quarters of the remaining dough, divide it into 65 equal pieces.

7 Roll out each piece into the shape of a torpedo and snip the edges of each one in the same direction to create ears of corn.

8 These ears of corn are placed onto the base of the wreath starting round the outer edge. On the inner circles, each ear should overlap the last. Place the last ears of corn over the tops of the stalks, to cover any uneven edges. Bake the wreath referring to the instructions on p.32.

9 Once baked and left to cool, colour-wash the ornament with yellow ochre and highlight for a high-baked effect. When the paints are thoroughly dry, varnish the Wheat Sheaf twice on each side for protection.

Tree

It is the simplicity of this tree which makes it such a timeless wall decoration. Instead of apples, you could decorate it with pears or even flowers.

MATERIALS

1 kg (2 lbs) dough (see Tips and Techniques, p.18)
flat-sided baking tray
rolling pin
sharp vegetable knife
pastry brush
ruler
cloves
poster paints: yellow ochre, burnt umber and scarlet
paint brushes
clear, satin varnish
linen tabs
strong adhesive
felt

METHOD

1 Using a piece of dough the size of a tennis ball, roll out a thick sausage shape 18 cm (7 in) in length.

2 Wipe the baking tray with a damp cloth and place the sausage shape onto it. The lower half represents the trunk, while the upper half will form a platform for the leaves.

3 Spread the lower half out slightly with your fingers and form it into the shape of a tree trunk. Use a knife to create a rough bark effect.

4 Using your fingers and then a rolling pin, flatten out the upper half of the tree to 6 mm (¼ in) thick – as a natural look is desired, it doesn't have to be completely symmetrical.

5 Using half the remaining dough, form a long sausage shape 1 cm (½ in) thick and cut 56 1 cm (½ in) slices, and make 56 leaves the same size (see Tips and Techniques, p.27).

6 Paint the base with water and place the leaves on it, starting with the outer edge and working inwards (see Wheatsheaf, p.78).

7 Leave small gaps for the apples and continue to cover the base with leaves.

8 Using balls of dough the size of horse-chestnuts, make as many apples as you need to give a look of abundance (see Tips and Techniques, p.30). The apples should nestle between the leaves.

9 When all the leaves and fruit are fixed into position, bake the Tree referring to the instructions on p.32.

10 Once the tree has thoroughly dried out it can be painted with a thin yellow ochre colour-wash. Then the trunk, edges of leaves and the apples can be highlighted with a high-baked effect (see Tips and Techniques, p.34). Finally, when dry, varnish your Tree twice on both sides.

11 To hang up your Tree, use a linen tab and cover the back with felt.

Pumpkin

For your next Halloween party try making this unusual wall plaque! It is easy to make, but also very effective, especially when painted.

MATERIALS

1 kg (2 lbs) dough (see Tips and Techniques, p.18)
flat-sided baking tray
rolling pin
small ovenproof bowl
15 cm (6 in) plastic ruler
sharp vegetable knife
poster paints: yellow ochre, cadmium yellow, scarlet and blue
paint brushes
clear, satin varnish

METHOD

1 Place the upturned bowl onto the baking tray and sprinkle it with flour.

2 Using three-quarters of the dough (750g/ 1½ lbs), roll out into a large circle, large enough to cover the upturned bowl. The dough should be at least 1 cm (½ in) thick.

3 Dust the underside of the dough with flour and place it over the bowl.

4 Carefully pat the dough into shape over the bowl with your hands. The pumpkin should be wider than it is tall and rather flat at the top and bottom.

5 Using the edge of the plastic ruler, make curved lengthwise indentations to represent the segments of a pumpkin. Slant the indentations towards the centre of the top and the centre of the base.

6 Make a very slight hollow in the base of the pumpkin with your thumb, as centrally as possible, pushing upwards into the dough.

7 Using the vegetable knife, cut out triangles to represent the eyes and nose. Make sure you cut right through the dough – it is advisable to use a gentle sawing action when cutting instead of pulling down with knife as this causes a jagged edge. Remove the cut-outs carefully. Cut out a large mouth with a jagged upper lip and a smooth lower lip. Remove the excess dough.

8 The stalk is made from a sausage shape 5 cm (2 in) long and 1 cm (½ in) thick, moulded carefully into the right shape. Make sure it adheres well to the pumpkin and bend it over slightly to the right. Bake the ornament (with the bowl still in position) referring to p.32.

9 After baking the pumpkin can be painted. Mix yellow ochre, cadmium yellow and scarlet, adding small amounts at a time until you achieve the pumpkin colour. The olive green is made by adding more yellow and a touch of blue to the orange colour already mixed.

Witch on a Broomstick

Bring something original to the next Halloween party you are invited to, or simply hang this decoration in your own home. She is quite easy to make – something perhaps for the children to attempt.

MATERIALS

1 kg (2 lbs) dough (see Tips and Techniques, p.18)
flat-sided baking tray
piece of doweling 6 mm (¼ in) wide and 19 cm
(7½ in) long (optional)
rolling pin
sharp vegetable knife
ruler
garlic press
pastry brush
poster paints: Halloween colours
paint brushes
gold felt tip pen

METHOD

1 Wipe your baking tray with a damp cloth. For the head, use a ball of dough the size of a horse-chestnut (conker). Place it on the upper half of the tray leaving space of at least 5 cm (2 in) at the top.

2 The body is made in three parts – the trunk of the body, thighs and shins – placed in a zig-zag on the tray, as shown. For the trunk of her body, make a sausage shape 6 cm (2½ in) long and 2.5 cm (1 in) thick. Place this under the head at an angle.

3 For the lower body and thigh make a sausage shape 7.5 cm (3 in) long and 2.5 cm (1 in) thick, positioned carefully at an angle (as shown in the photograph).

4 Before the shins, the broomstick must be added. To make it you can either use the piece of doweling, or if you can't get hold of

any it can be made out of a sausage of dough exactly the same size. Place the broomstick on the tray 5 cm (2 in) away from, but parallel to, the body.

5 Once the broomstick is in place make a sausage shape 7.5 cm (3 in) long and 1 cm (½ in) thick. Attach it to the end of the thigh piece for the shins. The knee and shin piece rest on the broomstick.

6 The pointed boot is modelled from a ball of dough the size of a cherry. The boot is rather long and pointed. Don't forget to make an indentation with a knife for the heel. Place the boot at the end of the shin, making sure it adheres well.

7 For the brush of the broom, use the garlic press to create long strands and finish with a thin strip of dough to represent the tie. Attach the brush to the broomstick.

8 The arm is a sausage shape 6 cm (2½ in) long and 1 cm (½ in) thick, bent in the middle and placed onto the body. The hand, which holds onto the broomstick, is made from an oval-shaped piece of dough. Make indentations for fingers with a sharp knife and carefully cut into the dough at one side to make the thumb.

9 The skirt, which only needs to cover the knee and shin is made from a rolled out rectangle of dough 11 cm (4½ in) long, 7.5 cm (3 in) wide, and 6 mm (¼ in) thick.

10 For the cloak, roll out some dough until it is 6 mm (¼ in) thick and cut out a shape 13 cm (5½ in) long, 18 cm (7 in) wide at one end and tapering to 7.5 cm (3 in) wide at the other. Using the pastry brush and water, wet the body of the witch. Try to gather the neck of the cloak and when placing it on the body, create folds to give the impression of movement in the wind.

11 Use a thin strip of dough for the bow around her neck (for bow, see Tips and Techniques, p.26).

12 The hair is made of strands of dough formed using the garlic press – it should look thick and wild.

13 The hat is made from a piece of dough the size of a small tomato. Pull it into shape as shown – the top of the hat should be thin and bent over. Finish it off with the brim. From a piece of rolled out dough 6 mm (¼ in) thick, cut out a strip 1 cm (½ in) wide and 6 cm (2½ in) long, and fix it right round the hat.

14 Make the nose from a small piece of dough pulled into shape, and finally finish off with the spider. This is a tiny ball of dough placed on her cheek. It can be left plain to represent a wart or be painted black to look like a spider.

15 This ornament will take around 3 days to bake – refer to the instructions on p.32.

16 Once baked, enjoy painting her and making her as evil looking as possible. Don't forget to varnish twice on both sides when the paints are thoroughly dry.

17 As a finishing touch add gold stars to the cloak and hat with a gold-coloured felt tip pen once the varnish is completely dry.

Christmas Tree Decorations

These Christmas Tree Decorations not only look lovely hanging on the Christmas Tree, but are also an ideal way of occupying the children during the festive holidays. You can make many different ones decorated with snowmen, angels, Father Christmas and so on.

MATERIALS

1 kg (2 lbs) dough (see Tips and Techniques, p.18)
2 flat-sided baking trays
a variety of biscuit cutters
sharp vegetable knife
garlic press
pastry brush
rolling pin
cocktail stick
poster paints: bright seasonal colours
paint brushes
gold felt tip pen
clear, satin varnish

METHOD

Start by choosing a selection of biscuit cutters or moulds in shapes that reflect Christmas time. Stars, moons and hearts, for example, make ideal basic shapes which you can then decorate in different ways and hang on your tree. A selection of design ideas are described below to get you started, but there are endless possibilities and you can really test your creative modelling skills. Miniature wreaths decorated with little berries, leaves, candles or flowers for example, or even pieces of fruit set on a single leaf, also make lovely alternatives to the more traditional Christmas ornaments.

1 On a floured work surface, roll out the dough until 6 mm (¼ in) thick, and using your cutters, cut out as many shapes as you can. Keep the excess dough out of the way to use later for decorating.

2 Wipe your baking tray with a damp cloth and carefully transfer the shapes onto it, making sure they are not placed too close to one another.

3 Decorate heart or diamond shapes with a little rose made from a piece of dough the size of a hazelnut, placed in the middle of two tiny leaves.

4 Once the flower and leaves are fixed in position, make a hole at the top of the heart using a cocktail stick.

5 When the decoration has been baked, paint the rose in a bright red colour wash and the leaves dark green. Add a red border all the way round the edge of the shape using undiluted paint. Varnish when dry.

6 Another idea is a star shape decorated with a little angel. Remember to make a hole at the top of the star for hanging.

7 For the angel's head, make a tiny ball of dough and flatten it slightly. Using the cocktail stick make three small indentations for the two eyes and the mouth. Place in position.

8 Mould a small piece of dough into a rounded triangle shape to represent the body. With the knife make several straight indentations to decorate, starting at the tip of the triangle and fanning out to the bottom. Fix the body under the head.

9 The two wings are two tiny triangles decorated with horizontal indentations, attached to side of the body beneath the head.

10 To make the angel's hair use four tiny balls of dough placed in a row around the top of the head, just above the eyes.

11 Once baked (see below), the angel should be painted in colours of your choice. Brighten the cheeks with a touch of pink and varnish the ornament once completed.

12 Little snowmen are also ideal for the Christmas tree. Make a small ball of dough for the head, and a slightly larger elongated ball for the body. Fix them together with a drop of water.

13 To decorate the head use tiny circles of dough for the two eyes, and a slightly bigger one for the nose. Make three holes in a row down the body to represent buttons.

14 The hat is made from a small rectangle of dough, rounded at the corners and fixed snugly around the top of the head. Finish with a brim made from a strip of dough, making sure that it touches the tray on either side.

15 Make the snowman's scarf with two strips of dough fixed at each side of the neck, and crossing each other round the front. The scarf is decorated with little straight indentations made with the knife.

16 Finally, make a hole in the hat for hanging, using the cocktail stick to pierce through the dough.

17 When it has been baked (see below), the snowman can be painted. The head and body can be left natural or painted white, the eyes and hat are painted black, the nose red, and I have chosen dark green for the scarf.

18 When you have finished modelling your decorations, they should be baked. Make sure they are not too close on the tray, and refer to the instructions on p.32. They should take about 24 hours to dry out in the oven.

19 Once thoroughly dry, each decoration should be painted. If any of them are in two parts, stick them together when the paints have dried using a strong glue, before varnishing. Varnish each piece twice on both sides.

20 Finish off by lacing string, ribbon or raffia through the holes leaving enough length so they are easy to hang on the tree.

21 Using horse-chestnut (conker) sized pieces of dough, shape into cones to make the bodies. Hazelnut-sized pieces of dough form the head and hair is made using the garlic press. Sausages of dough form the arms – leave the sleeve wide at the cuff. Strips of dough represent the rufflette. Small balls of dough form the hands and the hymn books are squares folded in half. The choir master is slightly larger.

Christmas Advent Wreath

This beautiful Christmas decoration can be used from the first Advent Sunday until after Christmas. It makes a beautiful table decoration and is just that little bit different.

MATERIALS

2 kg (4 lbs) dough (see Tips and Techniques, p.18)
flat-sided baking tray
pastry brush
rolling pin
ruler
sharp vegetable knife
4 night lights (candles)
poster paints: bright, seasonal colours
paint brushes
gold felt tip pen
clear, satin varnish
4 candles

METHOD

1 Using half the amount of dough (1 kg/2 lbs), make two sausage shapes 59 cm (23 in) long and 1.5 cm (1 in) thick. Use these to create the wreath (see Techniques, p.26).

2 Wipe over the baking tray with a damp cloth and transfer the wreath onto the tray. Decide where you want the four candles to go – it is advisable to put one over the join so that it will be hidden. The other three should be positioned at regular intervals so that the wreath will be symmetrical.

3 Take the four night lights (candles) and wet the base of the aluminium with water. Press each one firmly into the dough and remove the candles, leaving the holders embedded in the wreath. The holders should all be level with the surface of the dough.

4 Around each candle holder create a ring of holly leaves and berries. You will need to make 28 holly leaves in total, placing seven in a circle around each candle holder. To ensure that all the leaves are the same size, make a sausage shape 28 cm (11 in) long and 1.5 m (¾ in) thick, and cut into 28 1 cm (½ in) slices.

5 To make the holly shape, with your forefinger flatten each circle to a thickness of 6 mm (¼ in), then pinch both ends with thumb and forefinger to create two pointed ends. Pinch twice down each side, to make an elongated star-shape. Using a knife make an indentation down the centre from top to bottom.

6 Arrange the holly leaves around the candle holders, making sure they adhere well to the wreath. Be careful not to block the openings of the candle holders.

7 Once the leaves are all in place tiny berries can be made to cover any gaps in the rings of decoration (see Tips and Techniques, p.27).

8 For the bows, roll out the remaining dough on a floured surface until 6 mm (¼ in) thick, and cut four strips of dough 30.5 cm (12 in) long and 1.5 cm (¾ in) wide.

9 Create one bow with each of the strips (see Tips and Techniques, p.26).

10 Place the bows onto the wreath between each candle holder. Make sure they are secure, and that the ribbons flow onto the tray.

11 Bake the wreath referring to the instructions on p.32. Once thoroughly dried out, paint the wreath in bright seasonal colours, and when dry varnish twice on both sides. Add the finishing touches with a gold pen.

GIFTS

Fruit and Flower Swag

This pretty swag is painted with a thin wash of yellow ochre and then highlighted with a high-baked effect. It almost looks as though it has been carved out of wood and makes a beautiful centre piece on any wall or fireplace.

MATERIALS

1 kg (2 lbs) dough (see Tips and Techniques, p.18)
large flat-sided baking tray
3 bottle tops (sizes: 6 mm (¼ in); 1 cm (½ in);
2.5 cm (1 in) in diameter)
pastry brush
rolling pin
ruler
cloves
cocktail stick
tracing paper
thin card
scissors
poster paints: yellow ochre
clear, satin varnish
2 linen tabs (for hanging)
strong adhesive
felt

PREPARATION

Prepare the three templates for the swag from the back of the book (for method, see Tips and Techniques, p.24).

METHOD

1 Roll out the dough until it is 6 mm (¼ in) thick. Sprinkle its surface with flour and place the templates onto the dough. Cut out the three shapes with the sharp knife (see Tips and Techniques, p.24).

2 Wipe the baking tray with a damp cloth and place the shapes in the centre of the tray. The side pieces should fit neatly to the main piece. Use water to attach the pieces.

3 Make twenty leaves from cherry-sized pieces of dough (see Tips and Techniques, p.27).

4 Place eight leaves in a circle in the centre of the swag, leaving room for a large rose.

5 Place three leaves, forming a triangle, at the ends of the side pieces, leaving a 1 cm (½ in) gap in the centre for the apples. A further three leaves are each placed at the top of the side pieces, leaving a 2.5 cm (1 in) gap in the middle for the bows.

6 The four apples are made from pieces of dough the size of horse-chestnuts (conkers), using the cloves for stalks (see Tips and Techniques, p.30). These are shown as in the photograph opposite.

7 Decorate all the way round the edges of the swag with small berries (see Tips and Techniques, p.27).

8 Further leaves, in pairs, are placed around the swag, leaving gaps for fruit and flowers: two pairs on each side piece, and two pairs each side of the centre along the top of the swag.

9 For the roses, use rolled out dough 6 mm (¼ in) thick. For the large central rose cut out 4 circles using the 1 cm (½ in) bottle top, and 8 larger circles with the 2.5 cm (1 in) bottle top, and form the flower (see Tips and Techniques, p.28).

10 Four smaller roses are made in the same way using two 6 mm (¼ in) circles and five 1 cm (½ in) circles. Position on the swag.

11 The acorns are easy to make. Push a hazelnut sized piece of dough over the end of a pencil to form the cup. Place a small egg-shaped piece of dough in the cup. The acorns can be finished off using a cocktail stick to create a pitted effect on the cup.

12 Make the bows using rolled out dough 6 mm (¼ in) thick. Cut two strips of dough 20.5 cm (8 in) long and 1.5 cm (¾ in) wide. Mould them into bows (see Tips and Techniques, p.26). Add balls of dough to decorate. Bake the swag referring to the instructions on p.32.

13 When dry, paint in a yellow ochre colour wash and highlight the raised areas with a high-baked effect (see Tips and Techniques, p.34). Finally, varnish twice on both sides.

14 Fix linen tabs to the back to facilitate hanging, and cover the area with felt.

Fruit Wall Plaque

This triangular-shaped wall plaque is decorated with fruit, leaves and a pastry bow, and painted in blue and red colour washes.

MATERIALS

1 kg (2 lbs) dough (see Tips and Techniques, p.18)

flat-sided baking tray

sharp vegetable knife

pastry brush

rolling pin

ruler

cloves

poster paints: shades of blue, yellow and red

paint brushes

clear, satin varnish

METHOD

1 Roll out the dough 6 mm (¼ in) thick. Cut out a triangle 14 cm (5½ in) across at the top, and 16 cm (6½ in) in length. Wipe the baking tray with a damp cloth and place the triangle half way down and in the centre.

2 In the middle, 4 cm (1½ in) from the top, place a small circle of dough to form a platform for the grapes. Cover with balls the size of hazelnuts to form a triangular shape (see p.31).

3 Roll a sausage shape 2 cm (¾ in) thick, and cut nine 1 cm (½ in) slices to make the nine leaves (see Tips and Techniques, p.27). Place as follows: two either side of, and on a level with, the top of the grapes; the others placed symmetrically around the pointed end of the triangle. A gap is left below the top leaves for the apples.

4 The apples, pears and plum are made from balls of dough the size of horse-chestnuts (conkers), (see Tips and Techniques, p.30).

5 Make eight tiny leaves, using pieces of dough the size of hazelnuts and place them to fill any gaps (see Tips and Techniques, p.27).

6 Using the rolled out dough, cut a strip 30.5 cm (12 in) long and 4 cm (1½ in) wide, and form the bow (see Tips and Techniques, p.26).

7 Bake referring to p.32. When dry, paint with thin colour washes of blues and reds. Varnish twice on both sides.

Birds of Paradise

Using two different colours of dough, you can create this beautiful effect of contrast. The birds of paradise are very unusual wall decorations and would make a lovely gift for that friend of yours who has everything!

MATERIALS

1 kg (2 lbs) plain dough (see Tips and Techniques, p.18)

250 g (½ lb) brown-coloured dough (see Tips and Techniques, p.18)

flat-sided baking tray

pastry brush

sharp vegetable knife

rolling pin

cloves

cocktail stick

3 bottle tops (sizes: 1 cm (½ in); 1.5 cm (¾ in) and 2.5 cm (1 in) in diameter)

thin card and scissors

clear, satin varnish

linen tabs

strong adhesive

felt

PREPARATION

Prepare the templates for the birds of paradise, from the back of the book (for method, see Tips and Techniques, p.24).

METHOD

1 Roll out all the plain dough until it is 1 cm (½ in) thick, and sprinkle lightly with flour on its surface.

2 Place the two card templates onto the dough, not too close together, and cut out the birds with a sharp kitchen knife (see Tips and Techniques, p.24).

3 Pull away any excess dough and tidy the edges, softening the outlines with the help of the knife and your forefinger.

4 Wipe your baking tray with a damp cloth and transfer the birds onto it. Keep them as far apart as possible on the tray so you have room to decorate each one in turn without damaging the other.

5 To decorate the birds, using the brown dough make a sausage shape 5 cm (2 in) long and 1 cm (½ in) thick. Cut seven 6 mm (¼ in) slices, and mould each one into leaf shapes (see Tips and Techniques, p.27).

6 Use three leaves for the hen's crown, and three to make her tail. The remaining one should be placed in the centre of the chick's tail.

7 To enhance the beaks of both birds, using the brown dough cut out one small and one large triangle and fix over the beaks.

8 Roll out the rest of the brown dough until it is 6 mm (¼ in) thick. Cut out four circles using the 2.5 cm (1 in) bottle top. One circle is used for the hen's eye. The other three circles are decorated with indentations using a sharp knife and placed onto the bodies of the birds.

9 Using the 1.5 cm (¾ in) bottle top, cut out one circle for the chick's eye, and fix it carefully into place.

10 An oblong of brown dough covers the chick's crown. Make vertical indentations with a sharp knife.

11 Using both brown and plain dough, make numerous berry-shaped decorations to complete the detail on the birds (see Tips and Techniques, p.27). Don't forget to complete the eyes with small balls of plain dough, flattened with your finger. Follow the photograph of the finished birds for positioning.

12 To finish off, use cloves for the pupils and to enhance the chain-like decorations on the bodies of the birds.

13 Bake the birds referring to the instructions on p.32, and once dry and cooled, varnish them twice on both sides.

14 To hang up your birds, use small linen tabs and felt (see p.35).

Old Man

This comical figure is made using a combination of plain and brown dough to create effective colour variations. Only his face, the stripes on his waistcoat and his shoes have been painted after baking. Make his partner in the same way.

MATERIALS

500g (1 lb) plain dough (see Tips and Techniques, p.18)

500g (1 lb) brown dough (see Tips and Techniques, p.18)

flat-sided baking tray

pastry brush

ruler

garlic press

vegetable knife

cocktail stick

tracing paper

thin card

scissors

poster paints: your choice of colours

paint brushes

clear, satin varnish

PREPARATION

Prepare the collar and waistcoat templates from the back of the book (for method see Tips and Techniques, p.24).

METHOD

1 Using brown dough, make a sausage shape 14 cm (5½ in) long and 4 cm (1½ in) thick. Place it on the baking tray and flatten the shape slightly with your fingers.

2 At one end of the sausage, mould the tip with your fingers into the shape of gently-sloping shoulders.

3 Keeping the upper part rounded, flatten the dough slightly under the torso to enhance the chest and stomach area.

4 To form the legs, cut the bottom half of the sausage down the middle. Prise the legs apart slightly and pat them into shape to soften any hard edges.

5 Make two small oval shapes for the feet, still using the brown dough, and fix them to the base of the legs, pointing forwards.

6 Using plain dough, make a ball the size of a horse-chestnut (conker) for the head. Fix it to the top of the body.

7 Roll out the remaining plain dough until it is 6mm (¼ in) thick. Using the templates, cut out the two halves of the waistcoat and the collar (see Tips and Techniques, p.24).

8 Fix the collar first around the join between the head and the body. Make sure it goes right round so that its edges can be tucked under to touch the baking tray.

9 Repeat the same procedure for the two halves of the waistcoat, making sure they join neatly in the middle and the edges touch the tray.

10 Make a tie out of a thin strip of plain dough, and fix it in position under the collar. Using the knife, add little diagonal indentations along the length of the tie to give it texture.

11 Using the brown dough make two sausage shapes, 7.5 cm (3 in) long and 1 cm (½ in) thick. Flatten them at one end to form the cuffs, and taper the other ends to form the shoulders.

12 Fix the arms at the shoulders and curve them slightly. One arm lies at the side of the body so that the hand rests on the hip, while the other arm is bent at the elbow so that the hand rests on the chest.

13 Make two tiny ovals of plain dough for the hands. Before fixing them to the arms, cut into the dough to form the thumbs, and add three straight indentations next to each thumb to create the fingers.

14 Make a tiny ball of plain dough for the nose, and place it right in the centre of the face.

15 Press some brown dough through the garlic press to from tiny strands for the hair and mustache. Place a row of these around each side of the head, leaving a large bald patch at the top. Add the eyebrows leaving a little gap between them.

16 The moustache is made in the same way and fixed under the nose. Pinch each end to form tailored points.

17 Make five tiny balls of brown dough for the four buttons of the waistcoat and the knot on the tie. Before fixing them in position, make a hole in each with a cocktail stick.

18 The pipe is made out of a small strand of dough. Flatten the tip at one end and make a hole with the cocktail stick to create the bowl. Place it in the hand resting on the chest.

19 Bake the Old Man referring to the instructions on p.32.

20 Once thoroughly dry paint the face, the shoes and add stripes to the waistcoat in the colour of your choice. I have chosen to continue the colour theme with a darker shade of brown. However, you may choose to use a brighter colour to enhance the comical theme. Finish off by varnishing twice on both sides.

21 This figure can stand on a shelf leaning against a wall, but if you want to hang it up using linen tabs glued to the back of the head (see Tips and Techniques, p.35).

VARIATION

You could make a partner for the old man. Use brown dough for the body, arms, shoes and hair and before placing the arms, make a petticoat using white dough. Roll to a thickness of 6 mm (¼ in) and cut out a strip of dough 6 cm (2 ½ in) wide and 8 cm (3 in) long. It should just cover her shins. Make a lace effect using a cocktail stick. Her skirt, in brown dough, is 6 cm (2 ½ in) long. A collar and apron of white dough decorate the dress. Add a bow and buttons.

Egg Cups

These pretty egg cups make lovely gifts for both adults and children. They could be used to display a china or marble egg, or would be lovely at Easter for chocolate or painted eggs.

MATERIALS

To make two egg cups
500 g (1 lb) dough (see Tips and Techniques, p.18)
flat-sided baking tray
sharp vegetable knife
ruler
pastry brush
garlic press
1 egg
poster paints: your choice of colours
paint brushes
clear, satin varnish

METHOD

1 Wipe the baking tray with a damp cloth. Mould a small handful of dough into a smooth ball and place it onto your baking tray.

2 Press the egg gently into the soft dough to form the required indentation. Roll it around a little before taking it out, but do not press down into the dough too much as the cup should not be too thin underneath.

3 To decorate the egg cup, make a sausage shape 2.5 cm (1 in) long and 1 cm (½ in) thick and cut it in half. With each piece form a leaf (see Tips and Techniques, p.27).

4 Stick the leaves next to each other onto the side of the egg cup, leaving a gap in the middle for the daffodil and bud.

5 Make the daffodil (see Tips and Techniques, p.28), and position it onto the cup.

6 The bud is made from a small sausage shape, moulded as shown in the photograph opposite. Both daffodil and bud should nestle between the leaves.

7 Bake the egg cup referring to the instructions on p.32.

8 Once the ornaments are thoroughly dry, paint the daffodil and leaves with bright colours, and finish off by varnishing twice on both sides.

TIP

Try making other egg cups using different decorations, for example using tiny rabbits, chicks, lambs and other animals, or use other spring flowers such as primroses.

Painted Cock

This ornament makes a beautiful gift at any time of the year. It is very simple to make using the template, and can be painted in bright colours in a folk art style. Choose a brightly coloured ribbon for hanging it.

MATERIALS

1 kg (2 lbs) dough (see Tips and Techniques, p.18)

flat-sided baking tray

pastry brush

rolling pin

ruler

sharp vegetable knife

cocktail stick

2 bottle tops (sizes: 6 mm (¼ in) and 1 cm (½ in) in diameter)

tracing paper

thin card

scissors

poster paints: bright colours of your choice

paint brushes

clear, satin varnish

linen tabs

strong adhesive

felt

PREPARATION

Prepare the templates for the painted cock from the back of the book (for method see Tips and Techniques, p.24).

METHOD

1 Wipe the baking tray with a damp cloth. Roll out all the dough directly onto it so that it covers an area large enough to accommodate the templates, but making sure it remains at least 1 cm (½ in) thick.

2 Dust the dough with flour and place the templates onto the dough. Cut out the shapes carefully with a sharp vegetable knife (see Tips and Techniques, p.24), and pull away the excess dough.

3 Brush off any remaining flour from the shapes and tidy the edges with the edge of the knife so they are as smooth as possible. Press the upper edges with your forefinger to create a more rounded effect.

4 Using the pastry brush and water as adhesive stick the stand to the base of the ornament as shown.

5 Roll out a small amount of dough until it is 6 mm (¼ in) thick, and using the two bottle tops, cut out two different-sized circles. Use these to make the eye, sticking the smaller circle on top of the larger one, before positioning them onto the head.

6 A tiny thin sausage shape is placed above the eyes, and a small flat oval shape is used to decorate his neck.

7 To complete, decorate the stand and the "crown" of the cock with tiny balls of dough in the shape of small berries (see Tips and Techniques, p.27).

8 Bake the ornament referring to the instructions on p.32.

9 After baking and cooling, paint the cock in bright, eye-catching colours and, when thoroughly dry, finish off by varnishing it twice on both sides.

10 Finish off the painted ornament with a linen tab and cover the back with felt to enable it to hang on the wall (see Tips and Techniques, p.35).

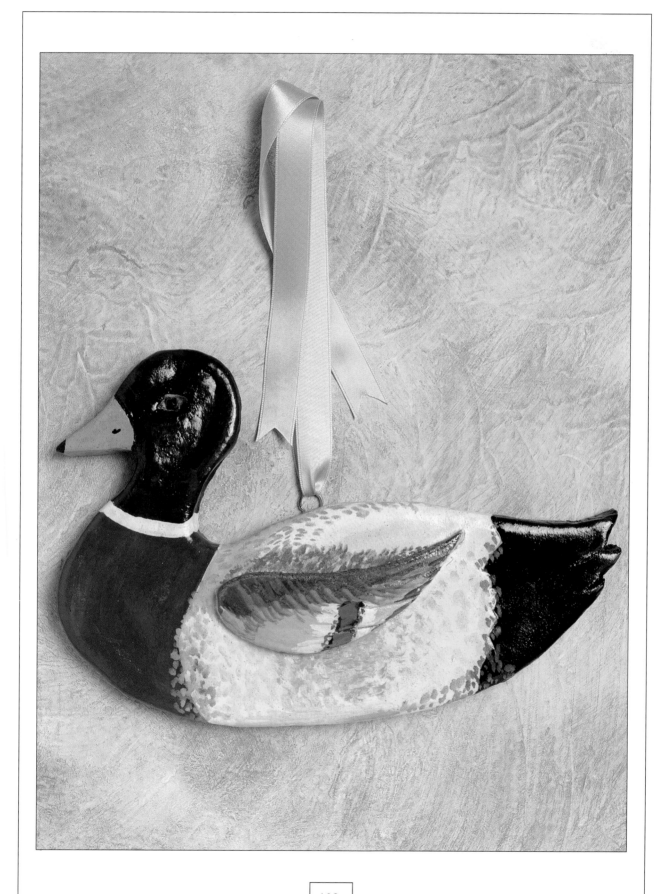

Mallard Duck

Ducks are very popular subjects for decorations. A salt dough duck as a wall plaque is something a little different however, and makes a lovely present. It is very simple to make and you can really put your painting skills to the test to make it as realistic as possible.

MATERIALS

1 kg (2 lbs) dough (see Tips and Techniques, p.18)
flat-sided baking tray
pastry brush
rolling pin
sharp vegetable knife
ruler
tracing paper
thin card
scissors
poster paints: colours of your choice
paint brushes
clear, satin varnish
linen tab
strong adhesive
felt

PREPARATION

Prepare the two duck templates from the back of the book (for method see Tips and Techniques, p.24).

METHOD

1 Wipe the baking tray with a damp cloth, and roll out the dough directly onto it until it is 1.5 cm (¾ in).

2 Sprinkle the dough with flour and place the template on the dough. Cut out the duck and the wing shapes (see Tips and Techniques, p.24), removing any excess dough.

3 Tidy the ragged edges of the shapes with the edge of the knife and gently press the upper edges with your forefinger to create a more rounded effect.

4 Fix the wing into position on the duck's body and attach.

5 Make the eye by pushing a clove into the soft dough in the desired place, making sure not to bury it in too far – it should remain clearly visible.

6 The duck is now ready to be baked. Refer to the instructions on p.32.

7 Once the duck is baked let it cool down very slowly, preferably turn off the oven and leave in there until cold. Larger flat surfaces can crack easily if they are cooled down too quickly.

8 The mallard duck should be painted in bright colours to reflect a natural look. Try using a photo or painting as a guide. When the paints are completely dry, varnish the duck twice on both sides.

9 Finish off the ornament with linen tabs and felt to enable it to hang on the wall (see Tips and Techniques, p.35).

Heart Plaque

This pretty heart-shaped plaque, decorated with spring flowers, would make a special gift for your valentine.

MATERIALS

1 kg (2 lbs) dough (see Tips and Techniques, p.18)
Flat-sided baking tray
Pastry brush
rolling pin
sharp vegetable knife
1 bottle top (size: 2 cm (¾ in) in diameter)
heart-shaped biscuit cutter (for variation)
paint brushes
poster paints
template
clear, stain varnish
ribbon

METHOD

1 Wipe the baking tray with a damp cloth. Roll out half the dough directly onto it until it is 1 cm (½ in) thick.

2 Dust the dough with flour. Using the heart-shaped template from the back of the book, cut out using a sharp knife.

3 Pull away any excess dough and neaten the edges with a knife or modelling tool.

4 Make a long, thin sausage of dough and position as a frame around the heart. Attach to the heart with water.

5 With a modelling tool or a cocktail stick, make two holes in the dough for threading ribbon through after baking.

6 Decorate the heart with a diagonal lines of primroses, daffodils and leaves (see Tips and Techniques, p. 27). Bake the heart referring to the instructions on p.32.

7 After baking, paint the frame and sides of the heart red and the flowers in bright colours. Finish off by varnishing twice on both sides and add aribbon for hanging.

VARIATION

This heart has been made in exactly the same way, except a heart-shaped biscuit cutter has been used to cut out the centre. Position two hazelnut-sized pieces of dough beneath the arches of the heart on either side. Make holes in the centre of each, piercing through the dough. Decorate with leaves and primroses.

Templates

These templates will help you with some of the more awkward shapes. The templates which have been reduced can be enlarged on a photocopier to bring them up to the correct size. The templates shown at the right size can simply be traced on to another sheet of paper.

Basket
This template can be used for any of the basket projects. Use a photocopier to enlarge the template to 130%.

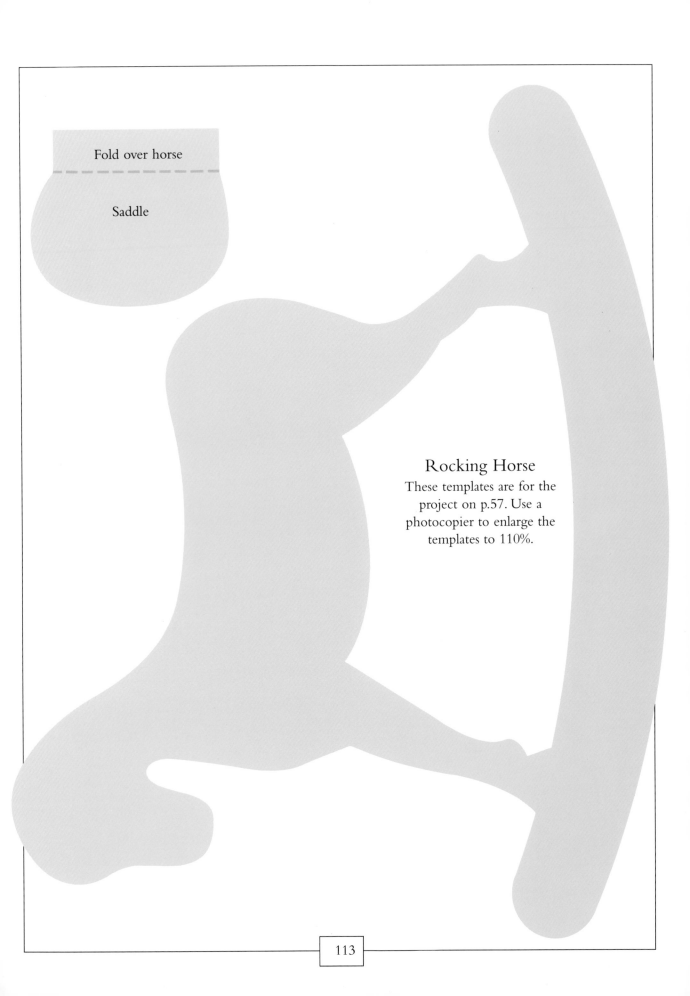

Fold over horse

Saddle

Rocking Horse

These templates are for the project on p.57. Use a photocopier to enlarge the templates to 110%.

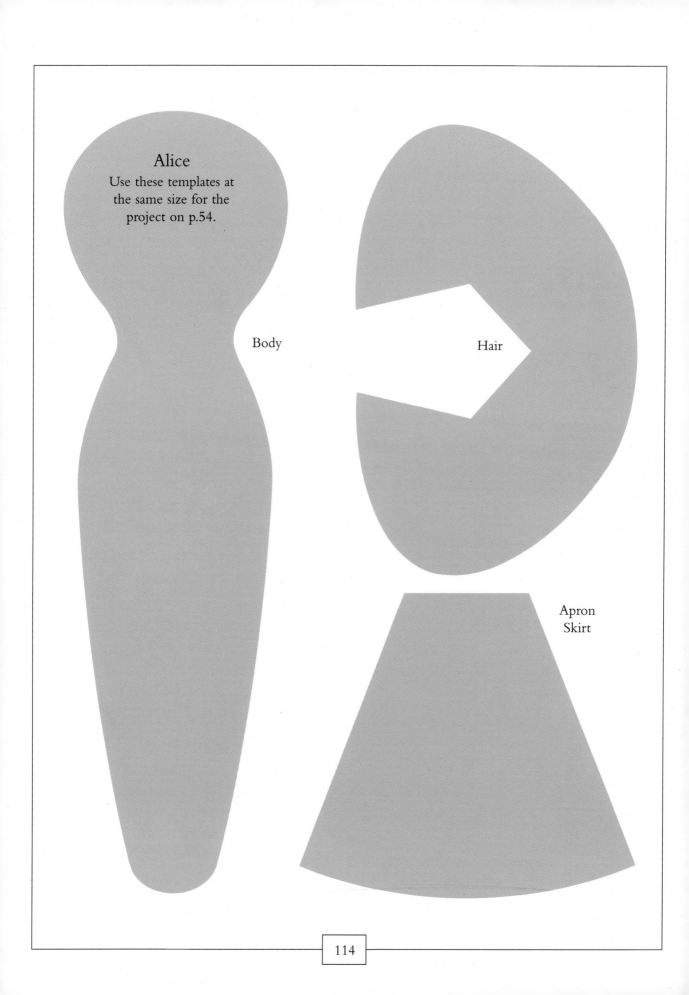

Alice
Use these templates at
the same size for the
project on p.54.

Body

Hair

Apron
Skirt

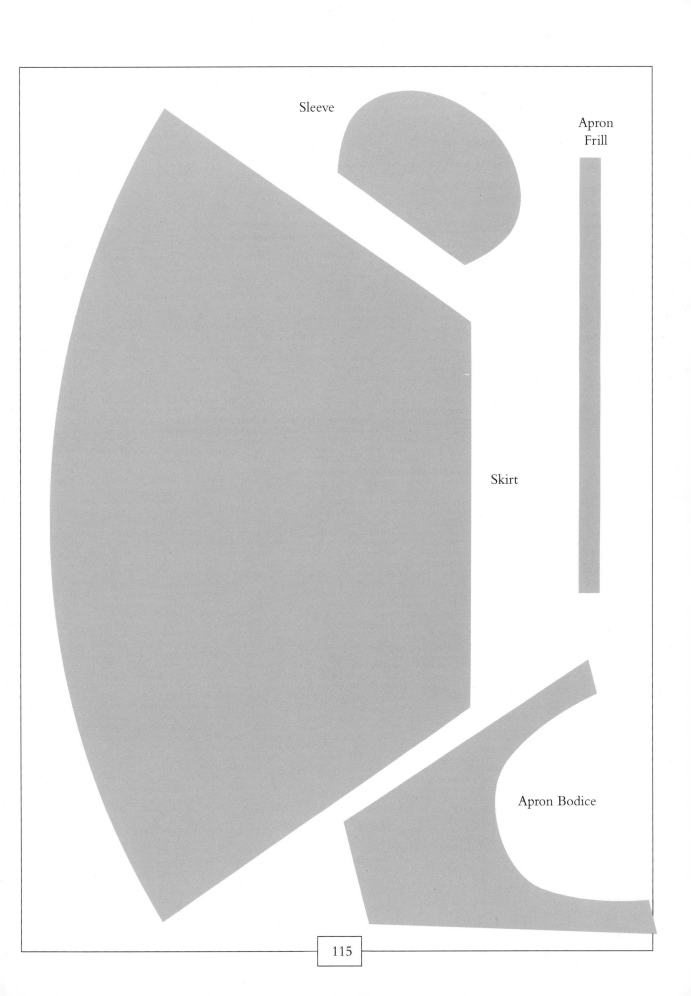

Sleeve

Apron
Frill

Skirt

Apron Bodice

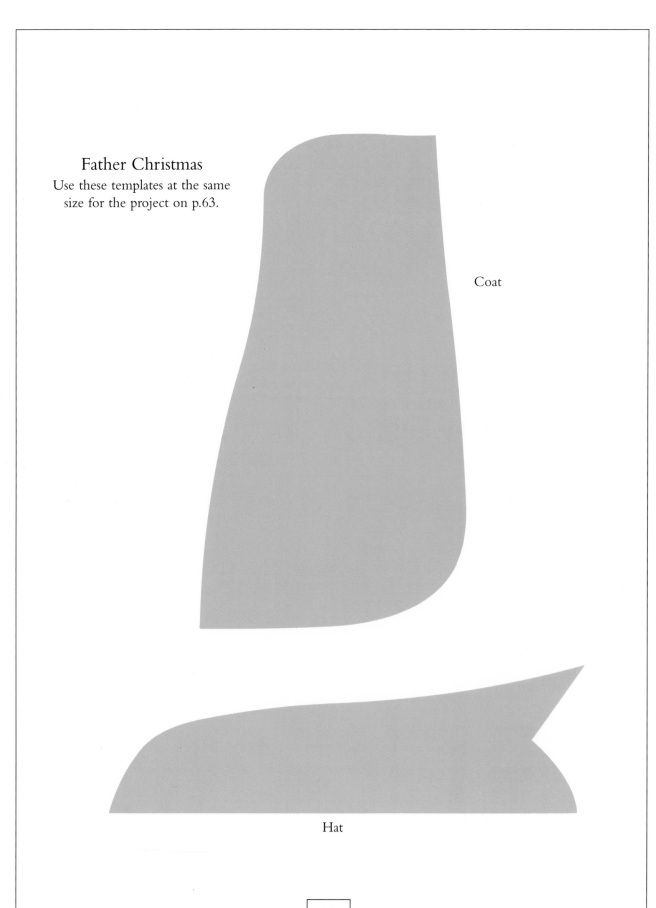

Father Christmas
Use these templates at the same
size for the project on p.63.

Coat

Hat

Cock

Cock and Hen
Use these templates at the same
size for the project on p.75.

Hen

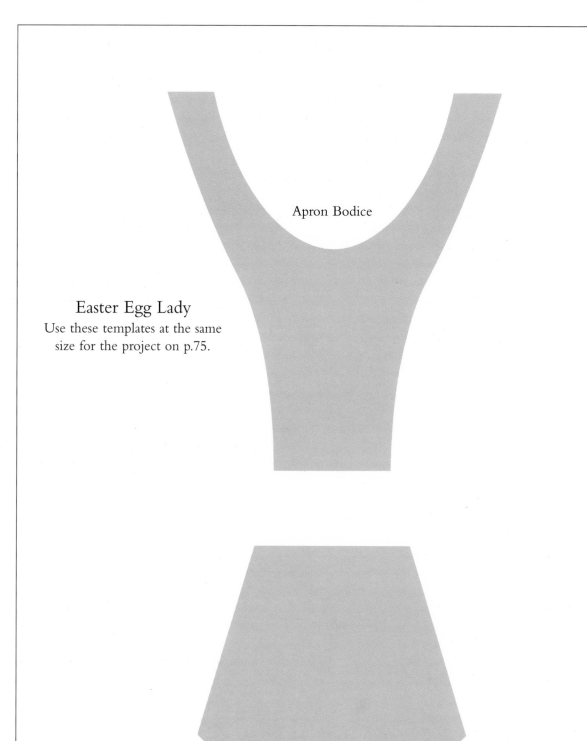

Apron Bodice

Easter Egg Lady
Use these templates at the same
size for the project on p.75.

Apron Skirt

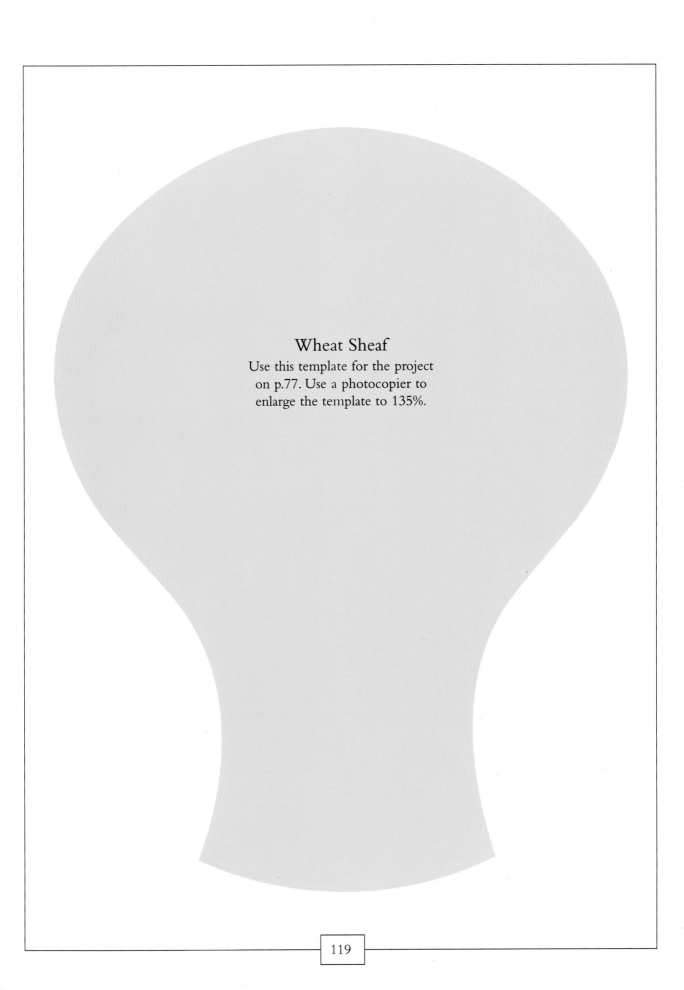

Wheat Sheaf
Use this template for the project
on p.77. Use a photocopier to
enlarge the template to 135%.

Swag

Fruit and Flower Swag
Use these templates for the project
on p.94. Use a photocopier to
enlarge the templates to 105%.

Top

Top

Right side piece

Left side piece

bottom

bottom

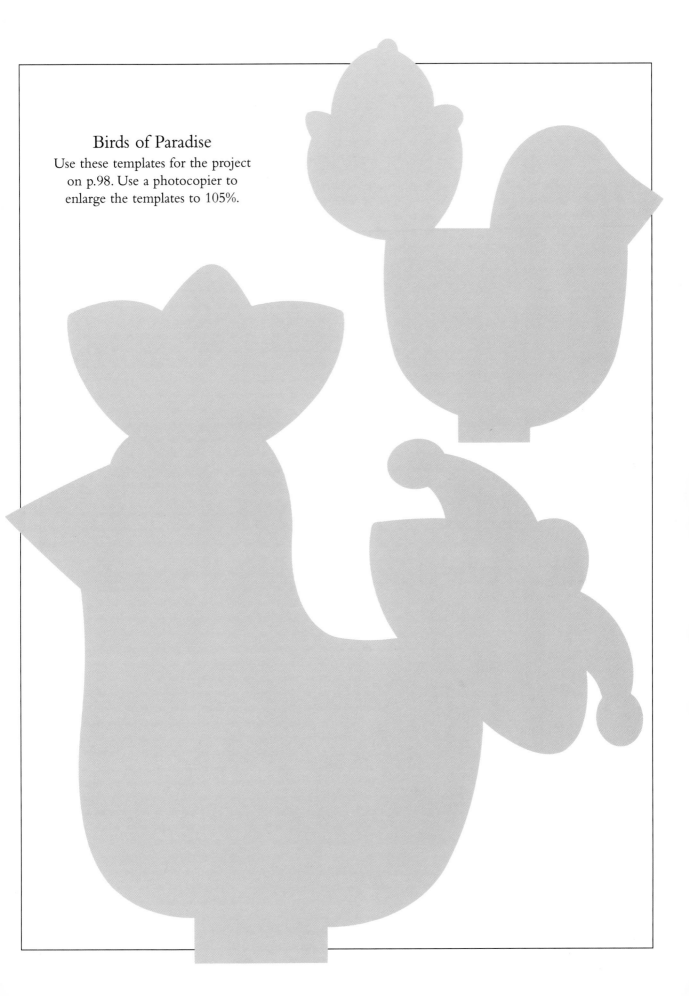

Birds of Paradise

Use these templates for the project on p.98. Use a photocopier to enlarge the templates to 105%.

Man's waistcoat
Cut one piece, then
turn template over
and cut again for the
other side of the
waistcoat.

Man's collar

Old Man
Use these templates at the same size
for the project on p.101.

Lady's apron

Lady's collar
Cut one piece, then
turn template over and
cut again for the other
side of the collar.

Painted Cock

Use this template for the project on p.106. Enlarge the template on a photocopier to 120%.

Stand

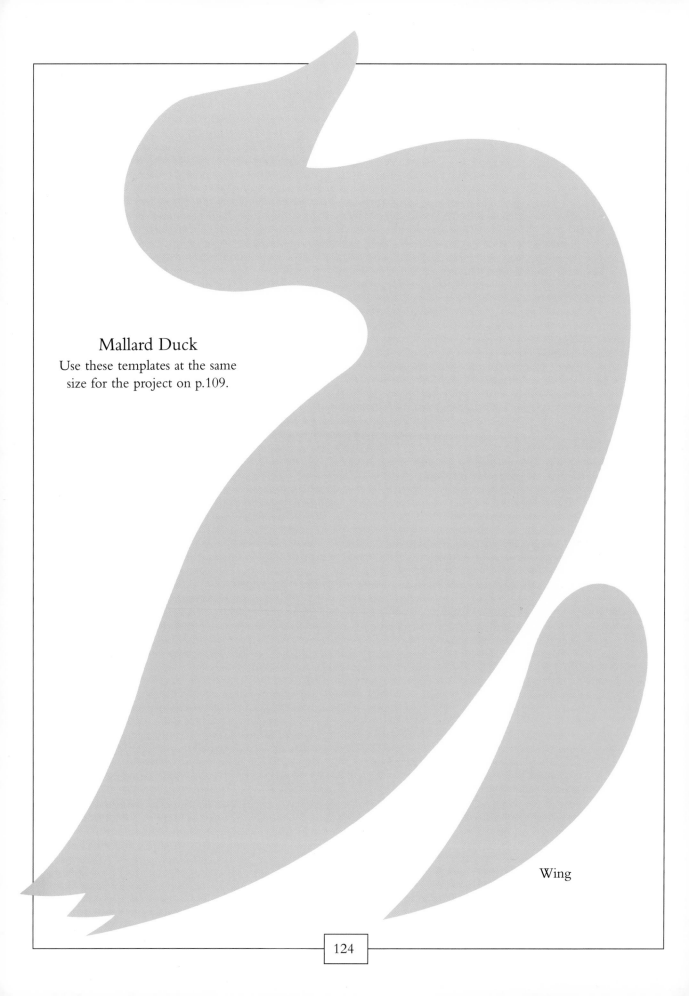

Mallard Duck

Use these templates at the same
size for the project on p.109.

Wing

Heart Plaque

Use this template at the same size
for the project on p.110.

Index

G000320205

Windows^xp

Davinder Singh Minhas

RISING SUN

RISING SUN

an imprint of
New Dawn Press

NEW DAWN PRESS GROUP
New Dawn Press, Inc., 244 South Randall Rd # 90, Elgin, IL 60123
e-mail: sales@newdawnpress.com
New Dawn Press, 2 Tintern Close, Slough, Berkshire, SL1-2TB, UK
e-mail: ndpuk@newdawnpress.com
         sterlingdis@yahoo.co.uk

New Dawn Press (An Imprint of Sterling Publishers (P) Ltd.)

A-59, Okhla Industrial Area, Phase-II, New Delhi-110020
e-mail: sterlingpublishers@touchtelindia.net
         Ghai@nde.vsnl.net.in

© 2005, New Dawn Press

All rights are reserved. No part of this publication may be reproduced,
stored in a retrieval system or transmitted, in any form or by any means,
mechanical, photocopying, recording or otherwise, without prior
written permission of the publisher.

Printed at Sterling Publishers Pvt. Ltd., New Delhi

Contents

Contents

1. Introduction

Windows^{Xp}

Microsoft Windows XP is the latest version of the Windows operating system. It is specifically designed for home computing and for big organizations. Windows XP provides with exciting experiences of the digital age at your fingertips. From digital photos, music and videos to building a home network, **Windows XP Home Edition** offers it all and takes you into the digital age with ease. Built on the solid foundation of Windows 2000, Windows XP also sets a new standard in efficient and dependable computing. A new visual design, reliable Windows engine, and new Internet security features combined with capabilities of computer sharing, make it the most dependable Windows operating system one has ever come across.

If home users or professionals have been waiting for one operating system that they could be fully happy with, it is probably the Windows XP, because it offers fastest speed and maximum stability. It offers complete freedom that users would like to experience with the computer and the Internet

Windows XP makes your computer significantly easier and faster to use than the earlier versions of Windows. Windows XP makes it easier to find information, files, and programs. It can accomplish tasks, such as customizing computer settings, using, storing and printing files and documents, faster. All this has been proven by extensive tests that were conducted by a reputed research laboratory.

Features of Windows XP Screen

The Windows XP screen displays various items, the presence of which depends on the setup of your computer.

My Computer

Displays all the folders and files stored in your computer.

My Document

Provides a convenient location to store your documents.

Title Bar

Displays the name of the open window.

Internet Explorer

Allows you to gain access to the Internet so that you can browse the Web.

Window

A rectangular panel on your screen that displays information and operates particular program.

Recycle Bin

Stores deleted files and allows you to recover them later.

Start Button

Gives you quick access to programs, files and Windows help.

Desktop

The background area of your screen.

Taskbar

Displays a button for opening each window on your screen. You can use these buttons to switch between the open windows.

Start Menu

The desktop will appear on the screen when you start your computer. By pressing the Start button on the desktop, you can open the Start menu and access programs, files and computer settings.

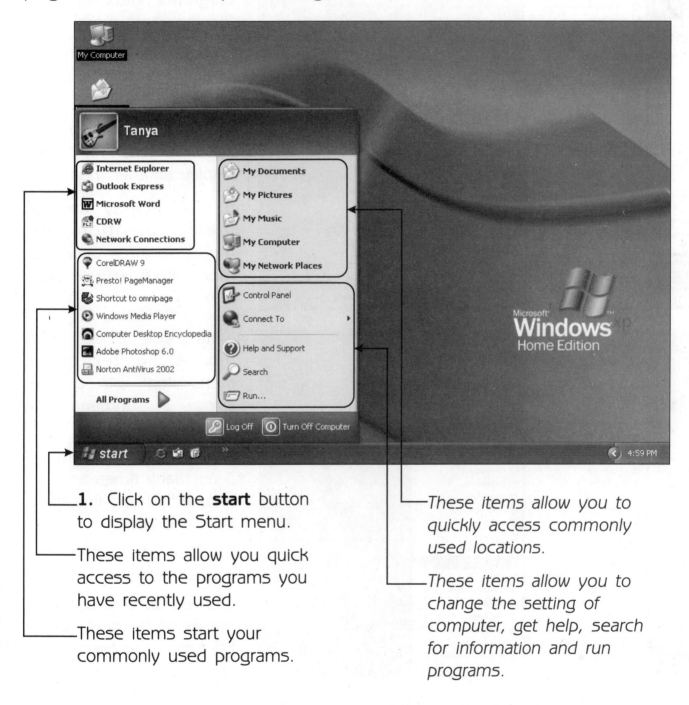

1. Click on the **start** button to display the Start menu.

These items allow you quick access to the programs you have recently used.

These items start your commonly used programs.

These items allow you to quickly access commonly used locations.

These items allow you to change the setting of computer, get help, search for information and run programs.

Many items can be seen displayed in the Start menu when it appears on the screen. You can click on the item you want to open in the Start menu.

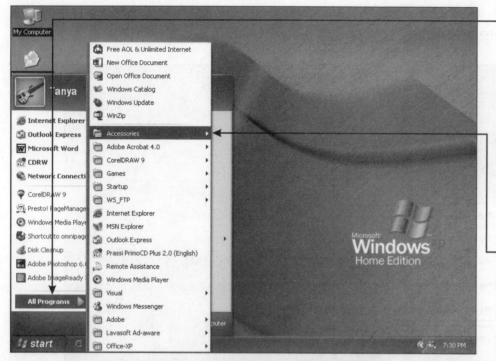

2. Click on the **All Programs** button to open the Programs menu.

A list of the programs appears on your computer screen.

A menu item with a side arrow on its right will display another menu.

3. To display another menu, position the mouse pointer over the menu item with a side arrow.

When you place your mouse pointer on a menu item with a side arrow, a submenu will appear.

4. You can repeat step 3 as many times as required till you find the item you want.

5. Click on the item you want to use.

Click on an area outside the menu to close the Start menu without selecting an item.

In this example, we open the Notepad window.

A button for the open window appears on the taskbar showing that the program is running.

Moving a Window

The window can be moved to another location, if it happens to cover an important item on your screen.

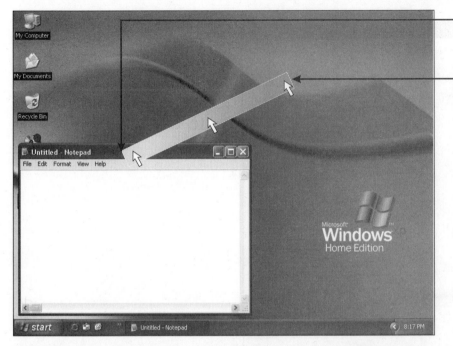

1. Place the mouse pointer over the title bar of the window you want to move.

2. Click and drag the mouse pointer to where you want to place the window.

The window moves to the new location.

Maximizing and Minimizing a Window

A window can be maximized to fill your entire screen. This allows you to view more information at once. If you are not using a window, you can minimize the window to temporarily remove it from your screen.

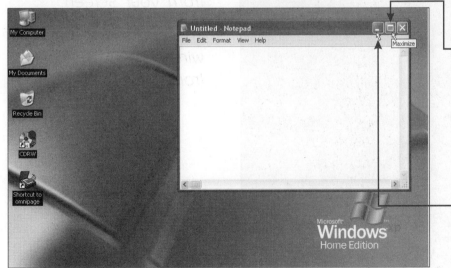

For maximizing a window

1. Click on the **Maximize** button (🔲) in the window you want to maximize.

The window fills your entire screen.

For minimizing a window

1. Click on the **Minimize** button (🔳) in the window you want to minimize.

The window reduces to a button on the taskbar.

To redisplay the window, click on its button on the taskbar.

Closing an Open Window

When you have finished working on the program window, you can close it to remove it from your screen. Closing of window will not close your computer.

1. Click on the **Close** button (☒) on the upper right corner of the window you want to close.

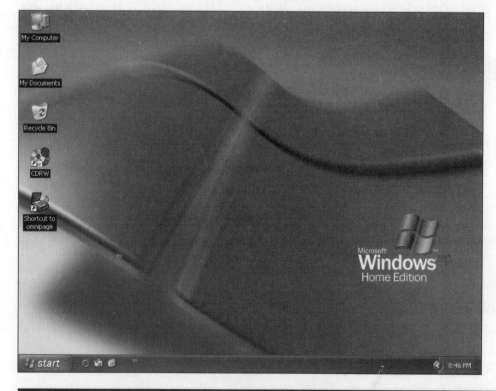

The window disappears from your screen.

The button for the window also disappears from the taskbar.

Shutting or Restarting Computer

Before turning off the computer, Windows must be shut down properly. And if your computer is not operating properly, you can also restart your computer.

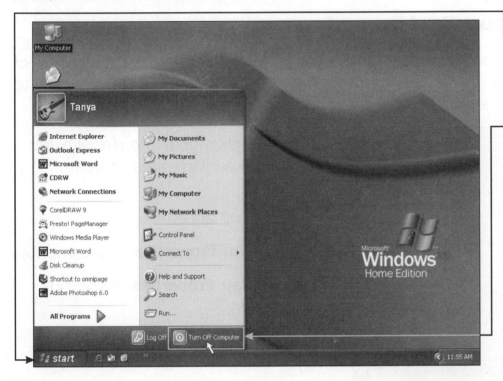

1. Click on the **start** button. The Start menu will appear.

2. Click on the **Turn Off Computer** button.

Before shutting down or restarting Windows, make sure you close all the programs that are running.

For Shutting Down

*The **Turn off computer** dialog box appears.*

3. Click on the **Turn Off** button to shut down Windows.

For Restarting

*The **Turn off computer** dialog box appears.*

3. Click on the **Restart** button to Restart your computer.

2. Customizing Windows

Changing the Desktop Background

You can select a picture, background color or both to enhance the appearance of your desktop. You can use your own picture or the picture that Windows provides to add a background to your desktop.

1. Right-click your mouse with the cursor on a blank area of your desktop.

A menu will appear.

2. Click on **Properties** in the menu.

*The **Display Properties** dialog box will appear.*

3. Click on the **Desktop** tab.

4. To display a picture on your desktop, click on the picture you want to use.

5. To select a background color for your desktop, click on the down arrow button of **Color:** to display a list of the available colors and select the color you want to use from the list.

6. This area displays a preview of the picture and desktop color you select.

7. Click on **OK** to add the picture or desktop color to your desktop.

The picture or color is displayed on your desktop.

Changing the Screen Saver

A screen saver is a computer program that usually displays various images on the screen of a computer that is on but not in use so as to prevent any possible damage to the computer screen.

1. Right-click your mouse with the cursor on a blank area on your desktop. A menu will appear.

2. In the menu, click on **Properties.**

*The **Display Properties** dialog box will appear.*

3. Click on the **Screen Saver** tab in the dialog box.

4. Click on the down arrow button of this area to display the available screen saver options.

5. Click on the screen saver you want to use.

6. This area displays a preview of the selected screen saver.

7. Double-click on this area and type the number of minutes to specify the time your computer must be inactive before the screen saver will appear.

8. Click on the **OK** button.

Changing the Screen Resolution

The amount of information that can fit in your screen can be adjusted by changing the screen resolution. The video adapter determines which resolutions are available on your computer.

1. Right-click your mouse with the cursor on a blank area on your desktop. A menu will appear.

2. Click on **Properties** in the menu.

*The **Display Properties** dialog box will appear.*

3. Click on the **Settings** tab.

4. To change the screen resolution, drag the slider to select the resolution you want to use.

5. This area displays a preview of the screen with the new screen resolution.

6. Click on the **OK** button.

Your screen will turn black for a moment.

Windows resizes the information on your screen.

*The **Monitor Settings** dialog box may appear.*

7. Click on **Yes** or **No** to specify whether you want to keep the new screen resolution.

*If you do not perform step **6** within 15 seconds, Windows will automatically restore your original screen resolution.*

8. You can also change the color quality of your screen from this option.

Changing the Mouse Setting

You can change the way your mouse works to make the mouse easier to use.

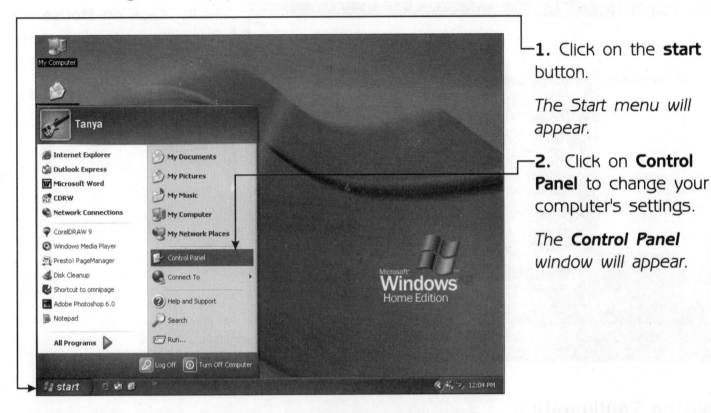

1. Click on the **start** button.

The Start menu will appear.

2. Click on **Control Panel** to change your computer's settings.

*The **Control Panel** window will appear.*

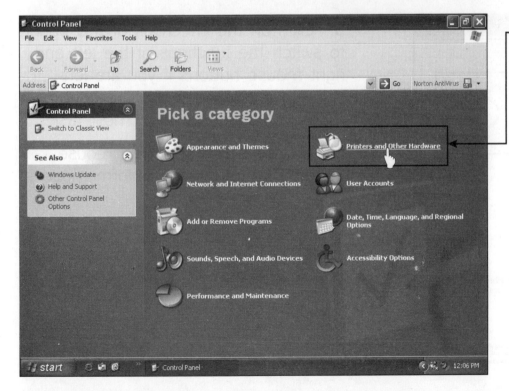

3. Click on **Printers and Other Hardware**.

The **Printers and Other Hardware** window appears.

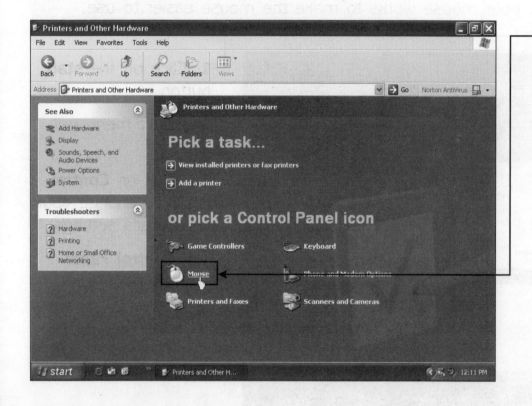

4. Click on **Mouse** to change your mouse settings.

*The **Mouse Properties** dialog box appears.*

Button Configuration

5. Click on the checkbox of this option to switch the functions of the left and right mouse buttons if you are left-handed, and want to use the right mouse button to perform most tasks.

6. This area displays which mouse button you will use to perform most tasks.

Double-Click Speed

The speed at which a mouse works can be personalized by changing the double-click speed.

1. Drag the slider to a new position to change the amount of time taken between two clicks of the mouse button for Windows to recognize a double-click.

2. Double-click on the folder in this area to test the new double-click speed.

The folder opens or closes according to the speed you select.

ClickLock

1. To select information or drag items without having to continuously hold down the mouse button, click on the checkbox in this option.

Pointer Appearance

You can change the appearance of the mouse pointers that Windows displays.

1. Click on the **Pointers** tab.

2. Click on the down arrow button of this area to display a list of the available mouse pointer sets.

3. Click on the mouse pointer set you want to use.

4. A list of mouse pointers included in the set you selected is displayed here.

The mouse pointer assumes different shapes. Each shape offers a visual cue to indicate what Windows is doing or the task you can perform.

Pointer Speed

You can also change the speed of movement of the mouse pointer on your screen.

1. Click on the **Pointer Options** tab.

2. Drag this slider to a new position to change the speed of movement of the mouse pointer on your screen.

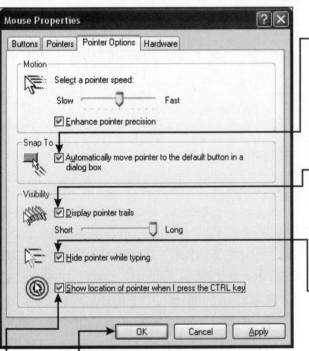

Snap To

1. Click on the checkbox in this area to make the mouse pointer automatically appear over the default button in most dialog boxes.

Visibility

1. Click on the checkbox in this area, to leave a trail of mouse pointers as you move the mouse pointer on your screen.

Hide Pointer while Typing

1. This option hides the mouse pointer while you type. To turn the option on or off, you can click on the checkmark in the checkbox in this area.

Show Pointer Location

1. Click on the checkbox in this area, to show the location of the mouse pointer whenever you press the **Ctrl** key.

2. When you finish changing the mouse settings, click on the **OK** button.

3. Windows Accessories and Games

Working with WordPad

What made the personal computer attractive was that one could type a document on it, save it, and then edit it later to correct grammatical errors and typing mistake without having to re-type the entire document. One cannot do these things on a typewriter.

Windows comes with a basic word processing program called **WordPad** that you can use to type, format, and print documents, such as letters and reports.

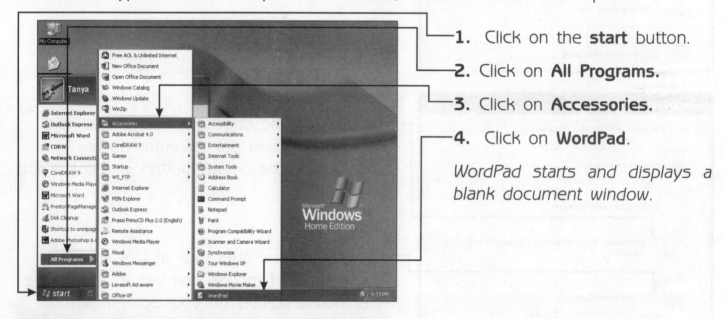

1. Click on the **start** button.

2. Click on **All Programs.**

3. Click on **Accessories.**

4. Click on **WordPad**.

   WordPad starts and displays a blank document window.

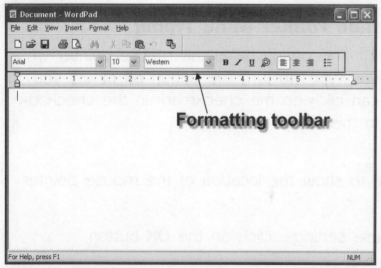

Formatting toolbar

5. Type your document in the blank window. You can use the drop-down lists and buttons in the Formatting toolbar to format the text as you type it.

Working with MS Paint

You can make use of the Paint tool to draw pictures. You can create logos for your business letters, create your own Clip Art and even paint pictures for your home or office. It is also useful for children as they can use this tool for preparing illustrations and drawing pictures for their classroom reports

When Paint is opened, it displays a blank page on which you can start drawing. You select the line or shape you want to draw from the Paint toolbox, choose a color, and then drag the mouse pointer over the page to draw the line or shape. You can create pictures or illustrations by using various shapes and colors.

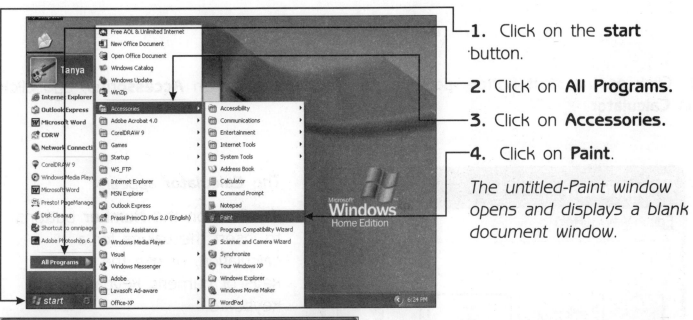

1. Click on the **start** button.

2. Click on **All Programs.**

3. Click on **Accessories.**

4. Click on **Paint**.

The untitled-Paint window opens and displays a blank document window.

5. You can draw images and edit them after opening Paint. You can draw lines, rectangles and free-hand images using different tools from the toolbar. You can also fill color in those images using the color palette.

Working with Calculator

For performing daily tasks, such as calculating the total due on a bill, we generally use a calculator. The Windows Calculator is much convenient to use. You can always access it from the **start** > **All Programs** > **Accessories** menu.

It is easy to use the Window calculator as it functions like any other simple calculator. You click on the number buttons to enter values and then you use the add, subtract, multiply or divide button to perform common mathematical calculations. However, the Calculator buttons do look a bit different from the buttons you find on an ordinary calculator.

1. Click on the **start** button, point to **All Programs** and then **Accessories**, and click on **Calculator**.

*The **Calculator** appears.*

2. Click on the **Number** buttons to insert the values for a calculation, or use the number keys or numeric keypad of the keyboard.

Playing Games on Windows

Windows is not all about performing business tasks. When you need a break from the daily grind, you can play any of the several Windows games.

1. To start a game, click on the **Start** button, point to **All Programs,** then **Games** and click on the game you want to play. Given below are some of the games you can play on your computer.

Free Cell

This is reverse Solitaire (see page 20). You start with eight stacks of cards all face up, four free cells and four home cells. The object of the game is to use all the cards to the home cells, using the free cells as placeholders. To win, you must have four stacks of cards on the home cell, stacked in order of rank, from the highest to the lowest.

Hearts

It is a multi-player game designed to be played on a network. In Hearts, the person with the lowest score wins. You try to give your Hearts (each worth one point) and the Queen of Spades (worth 13 points) to the other players, or you try to win all the Hearts and the Queen of Spades to score zero and penalize the other players 26 points each.

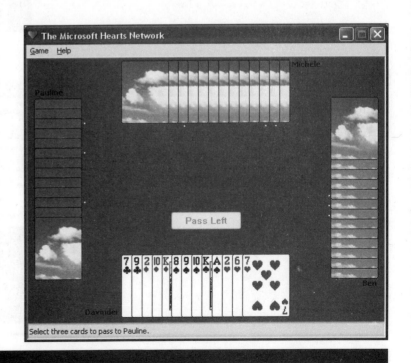

Minesweeper

Minesweeper is a game of strategy in which several mines are hidden under a grid of tiles. The aim is to avoid clicking on those tiles under which mines may be hidden. If you uncover a mine, you lose the game.

Pinball

Pinball is the similar pinball game you find at an arcade. You launch a ball and then try to score as many points as possible.

Solitaire

Solitaire is a classic card game that you play on your own. The object of the game is to use all the cards in the desk to build up the four suit stacks in ascending order, beginning with the aces

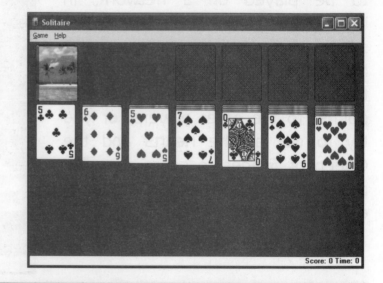

4. Working with Files and Folders

Viewing Personal Folders

Windows makes it a lot easier to place your files and manage them at the same time. The files can be viewed any time.

My Documents is your personal folder. It contains two specialized personal folders—My Pictures and My Music. You can make your personal folders available to others, or keep them as private so that only you can access the files within them.

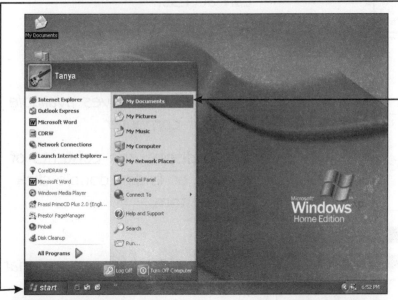

1. Click on **start.** The Start menu will appear.

2. Click on **My Documents** to view your documents.

The My Documents folder window will appear displaying its contents. This folder is useful for storing documents such as letters, reports and memos. My Documents folder contains many other folders in it.

This area displays all the files and folders.

This area displays options you can select to work with the documents in the folder.

3. You can close My Documents folder by clicking on the **Close** button (**x**).

Viewing My Computer

You can simply browse through the drives, folders and files on your computer. Windows uses folders to organize the information stored on your computer.

1. Click on **start**. The Start menu will appear.

2. Click on **My Computer** to open My Computer for viewing the contents of your computer.

The folders in this area contain files that all users connected to your computer can access.

The items in this area represent your hard drive, floppy drive, CD-ROM drive and any other drives available on your computer.

3. To display the contents of a drive or folder, double-click on the item.

This area displays options that you can select to perform common tasks and access commonly used locations on your computer. The available options depend on the selected item.

The contents of the drive or folder you select appears in this area.

4. You can browse through the contents of your computer or double-click on a folder to display its contents.

Click on the **Back** button ( ) on the toolbar to return to a window you previously viewed.

5. Click on the **Close** button (**x**) to close the window once you finish viewing the contents of your computer.

Changing the View of Folders and Files

You can even change the view of folders and files in a window. The view you select determines the way the files and folders will appear in the window.

1. Click on **View** on the menu bar to change the view of the contents in the window.

A bullet (•) appears beside the current view of the items.

2. Click on the way you want to view the items.

*This is an example of a detailed view as the **Details** option has been selected in this case.*

Types of Views

Filmstrip: This view displays pictures in a single row that you can scroll through. This view is only available in some windows, such as My Pictures window. A larger version of the picture can be viewed by clicking on it.

Thumbnails: The Thumbnails view displays a miniature version of picture files and some other types of files. If a miniature version of a file cannot be shown, an icon is displayed to indicate the type of file, as in the case of a WordPad document. In this view, miniature versions of a few pictures within a folder are shown on the folder's icon.

Tiles: The Tiles view displays items as large icons and information about each item is given below the item's file name. You can sort the items and change the information that each item displays.

Icons: The Icons view displays items as small icons with the file name appearing below each icon.

List: The List view displays items as small icons arranged in a list. This view is useful if you want to find a particular item in a long list of items.

Details: The Details view displays information about each item including its name, size, type and the date when it was last modified.

Sorting the Items

You can sort the items displayed in a window to be able to gain a quick access to files and folders.

1. Click on **View**.

2. Click on **Arrange Icons by**.

3. Click on the type of sorting you want for the items in the window.

*The items appear in a new order after being sorted by **Type** in this example.*

You can only sort the items in the reverse order when viewing them in the List or Details view.

Windows Explorer

You can view the files and folders on your computer with Windows Explorer.

The hierarchical structure of files, folders and drives on your computer is displayed by Windows Explorer. You can copy, move, rename and search for files and folders in Windows Explorer. For example, you can open a folder that contains a file you want to copy or move, and then drag the file to another folder or another drive.

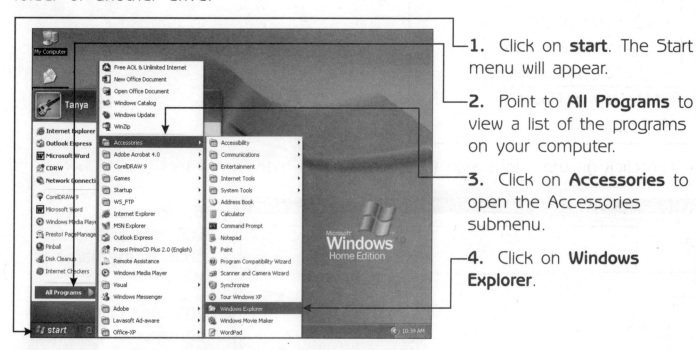

1. Click on **start**. The Start menu will appear.

2. Point to **All Programs** to view a list of the programs on your computer.

3. Click on **Accessories** to open the Accessories submenu.

4. Click on **Windows Explorer**.

Windows Explorer appears.

This area displays the list of folders on your computer.

A folder displaying a plus sign (+) contains hidden folders.

5. Click on the plus sign (+) beside the folder to display the hidden folders within that particular folder.

The hidden folders appear.

The plus sign (**+**) beside the folder changes to a minus sign (-). This indicates that all the hidden folders have been displayed.

You can click on the minus sign (-) to once again hide the folders.

6. To display the contents of a folder, click on the name of the folder.

This area displays the contents of the folder.

7. Click on the **Close** button (**×**) to close the window after you finish using Windows Explorer.

If you have worked with Windows Explorer (or My Computer) in Windows 95, the biggest improvement you will notice here is that the toolbar is different. To make your computer as easy to navigate as the World Wide Web, Microsoft redesigned the toolbar by adding the Back and Forward buttons that allow you to gain quickly access to the previous folder or disk. The toolbar also contains an Address text box/drop-down list into which you can type the path to a folder. Windows Explorer can also be used to open and display Web pages.

Selecting Files or Folders

Before working with files, you often need to select the ones you want to work with. Selected files appear highlighted on your screen.

To Select One File

1. Click on the file you want to select. The file gets highlighted.

2. Click on **Details** in this area to display information about the file.

Information about the file appears, including the file type and the date and time on which the file was last modified.

Click on **Details** again, to hide the information.

To Select a Group of Files

1. Click on the first file you want to select.

2. Press and hold down the **Shift** key as you click on the last file you want to select.

To Select Random Files

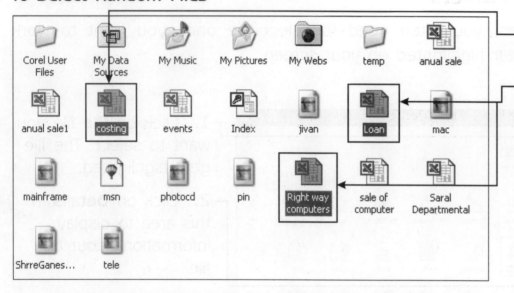

1. Click on a file you want to select.

2. Press and hold down the **Ctrl** key as you click on each file you want to select.

To Select All the Files

1. Click on **Edit** to select all the files and folders in a window.

2. Click on **Select All** in the Edit menu.

All the files and folders get selected.

Opening a File

Opening a file allows you to review and make changes to the file. You can open folders the same way you open files.

1. Double-click on the file you want to open.

The file opens. You can now review and make changes to the file.

If you open a picture, the picture appears in the Windows Picture and Fax Viewer window.

2. Click on the **Close** button **(x)** to close the file, after you finish working on it.

Deleting a File or Folder

The files or folders that you no longer need can be deleted to save hard disk space in your computer.

1. Click on the file you want to delete.

To delete more than one file, select all the files you want to delete.

2. Click on **Delete this file** or press the **Delete** key on the keyboard.

*The **Confirm File Delete** dialog box appears.*

3. Click on **Yes** to delete the file. The file disappears and is sent to the Recycle Bin.

Windows places the file in the Recycle Bin in case you want to restore the file later.

You can easily restore any file from the Recycle Bin to its original location on your computer because the Recycle Bin stores all the files that you have deleted.

You can also empty the Recycle Bin to create more free space on your computer. The files are permanently removed and cannot be restored if you delete them from the Recycle Bin and make it empty.

To delete a folder from your computer, right-click on the folder name and click on the delete button in the menu.

5. Windows Media Player

Windows Media Player (WMP) is used to play many kinds of audio and video files. WMP opens by default whenever you click on any sound or video icon.

1. Double-click on the audio or video file you want to play.

*The **Windows Media Player** window appears.*

This area displays the visual of the video you select.

If you select a sound file, the sound is played. This area may display a graphical representation of the sound.

Seek slider indicates the progress of the audio or video file.

2. Click on the **View Full Screen** button to see the full screen view of the video.

*The video continues to play in the full screen view. Press the **Esc** key on the keyboard to display the video in a window again.*

You can adjust the volume with this slider.

You can mute the sound with this button.

You can pause or stop the play of the audio or video file with these buttons.

*You can close the Windows Media Player window by clicking on the **Close (x)** button.*

Playing Music CDs

Nowadays, computer is not meant only for work. You can enjoy playing music CDs on your computer while you work. You need a computer with sound facilities and a CD-ROM drive to play music CDs.

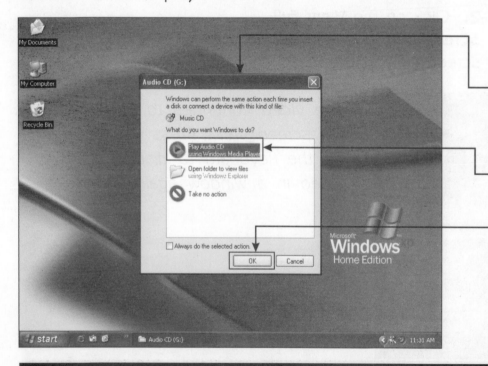

1. Insert a music CD into your CD-ROM drive.

*The **Audio CD** dialog box appears with options for you to choose from.*

2. Click on this option to play the music CD.

3. Click on the **OK** button.

The **Windows Media Player** window appears and starts playing the track.

—A list of the songs on the CD and the duration of each track gets displayed in this area. The song currently playing is highlighted.

—To play a specific song in the list, double-click on the song.

—Use these buttons to play the **next** song or to play the **previous** song.

—This area displays the length of time the current song has been playing for.

—You can click on the shuffle button to play the songs on the CD in a random order. Click on the shuffle button once again to play the songs in their proper order.

4. When you finish listening to the CD, click on the **Close** button **(x)** to close the Windows Media Player window.

5. Remove the CD from your CD-ROM drive.

6. Optimizing Performance

Viewing Disk Space

You can view the amount of space used and the amount that is free on a disk. You should check the free space on your computer's hard disk regularly.

1. Click on **start**. The start menu will appear.

2. Click on **My Computer**.

The My Computer window appears.

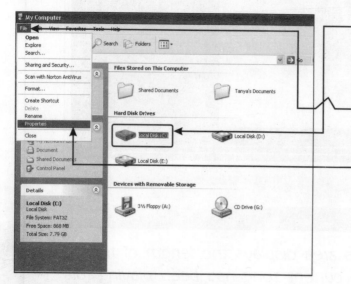

3. Click on the disk of interest, to view the amount of space on a disk for example Local disk (C:).

4. Click on **File**. The File menu will appear.

5. Click on **Properties**.

The Properties dialog box appears.

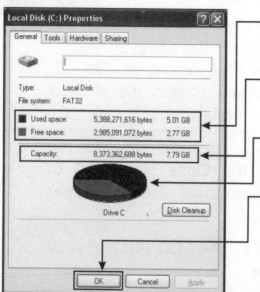

This area displays the amounts of used and free space on the disk in bytes and gigabytes (GB).

This area displays the total disk storage space, in both bytes and gigabytes (GB).

The Pie chart displays the amounts of used and free space on the disk.

6. Click on **OK** to close the **Properties** dialog box when you have finished reviewing the information.

Using Disk Cleanup

Over a period of time, many unwanted files get accumulated in your computer. You can use the **Disk Cleanup** option to remove such files.

1. To open Disk Cleanup, Click on **start > All Programs > Accessories > System Tools** and then click on **Disk Cleanup**.

This area displays the total amount of disk space you can free up.

This area displays the types of files Windows can delete and the amount of disk space each file type uses.

2. Windows will delete the files that displays a checkmark beside them. You can click on the box beside a file type to add or remove a checkmark.

3. Click on **OK** to delete the files.

A **dialog box** appears, confirming that you want to delete the files. Click on the **Yes** button to permanently delete the files.

Using Disk Defragmenter

Defragmenting your hard disk will make your programs run faster and your files open quicker. It will increase the lifespan of your hard disk. You should defragment your hard disk at least once a month.

1. Click on **start**. The start menu will appear.

2. Click on **All Programs** to view a list of the programs on your computer.

3. Click on **Accessories** in the All Programs menu.

4. Click on **System Tools** in the Accessories menu.

5. Click on **Disk Defragmenter**.

*The **Disk Defragmenter** window will appear.*

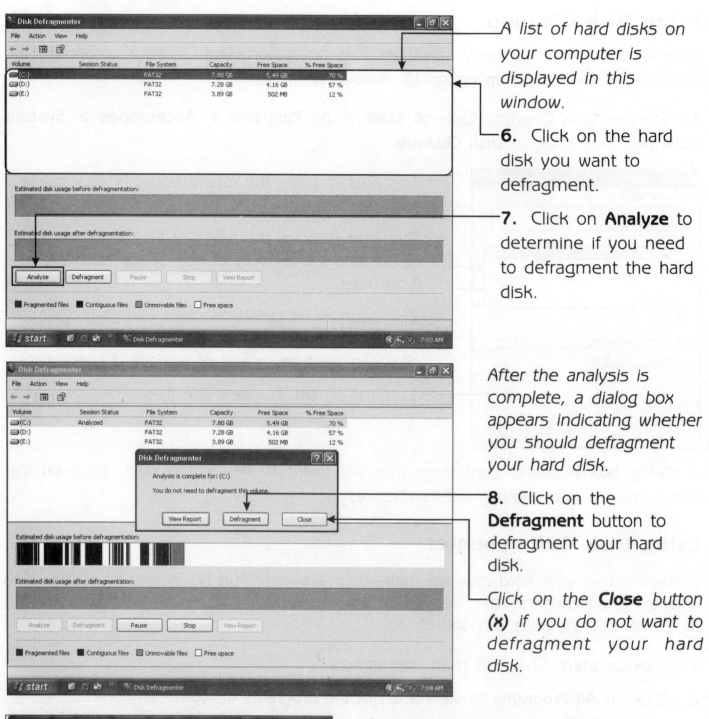

A list of hard disks on your computer is displayed in this window.

6. Click on the hard disk you want to defragment.

7. Click on **Analyze** to determine if you need to defragment the hard disk.

After the analysis is complete, a dialog box appears indicating whether you should defragment your hard disk.

8. Click on the **Defragment** button to defragment your hard disk.

*Click on the **Close** button (**x**) if you do not want to defragment your hard disk.*

A dialog box appears when the defragmentation is complete.

9. Click on the **Close** button (**x**) to close the dialog box.

10. Click on the **Close** button to close the **Disk Defragmenter** window.